WEST LAFAYETTE PUBLIC LIBRARY

W9-BRT-992

641
.597
GEL

Gelber, Irwin,
1933-
    The
international
kitchen
    Mexico Central

1/05

West Lafayette Public Library
West Lafayette, Indiana

THE INTERNATIONAL KITCHEN

THE INTERNATIONAL KITCHEN

Mexico, Central America, South America, and the Caribbean

IRWIN GELBER

VAN NOSTRAND REINHOLD
——————————— New York

West Lafayette Public Library
West Lafayette, Indiana

Copyright © 1993 by Van Nostrand Reinhold

Library of Congress Catalog Card Number   90-44224
ISBN 0-442-31939-8

All rights reserved. No part of this work covered by the copyright hereon may
be reproduced or used in any form by any means — graphic, electronic, or
mechanical, including photocopying, recording, taping, or information storage
and retrieval systems — without written permission of the publisher.

Printed in the United States of America

Van Nostrand Reinhold
115 Fifth Avenue
New York, New York 10003

Chapman and Hall
2 – 6 Boundary Row
London, SE1 8HN, England

Thomas Nelson Australia
102 Dodds Street
South Melbourne 3205
Victoria, Australia

Nelson Canada
1120 Birchmount Road
Scarborough, Ontario MIK 5G4, Canada

16 15 14 13 12 11 10 9 8 7 6 5 4 3 2 1

Library of Congress Cataloging-in-Publication Data

Gelber, Irwin
  The international kitchen.

  Includes bibliographical references and indexes.
  Contents: v. 1. Europe, the Mediterranean, the
Soviet Union, and Scandinavia — v. 2. The cuisines
of Latin America.
  1. Cookery International.   I. Title.
TX723.5.A1G45   1991   641.59   90-44224
IBSN 0-442-31939-8

CONTENTS

LIGHT DISHES AND APPETIZERS   23

SOUPS   47

BEANS, RICE, AND OTHER STARCHES   73

FISH AND SEAFOOD   89

CHICKEN   121

MEATS 143

VEGETABLES AND SALADS   185

DESSERTS   209

PREFACE

The second volume of *The International Kitchen* seeks to provide the professional chef and the serious student of the culinary arts with a selection of dishes reflecting the culinary heritage of Latin America, serving to stimulate the desire to learn more about the foods from this part of the world, provide a catalyst for culinary innovation and creativity, and, last but not least, satisfy the needs of those who partake of our efforts, our guests.

We live in an era in which people are able to move freely from one country to another, carrying with them the traditions of their native cultures. Today's multicultural societies enjoy expanded taste preferences and a heightened curiosity about food. Moreover, their awareness serves to guide culinary efforts away from parochialism and toward the development of more "globally conscious" menus.

This volume is devoted to the culinary heritage of Mexico, the Caribbean, and Central and South America. The preparations presented in this volume are rooted, for the most part, in the cuisine of the common people, comprising a collection of representative appetizers, soups, beans and rice dishes, and desserts, as well as fish, poultry, and meat entrées. As in the first volume of *The International Kitchen*, the recipes reflect a commitment to the use of fresh, easily obtainable ingredients and a straightforward, uncomplicated style of preparation. In making a selection it was difficult, at times, to pinpoint the exact origin of a particular preparation, since several similar in concept and content appear in a number of different countries.

At best, recipes serve as a guide for the creative cook. Innovative variations, however, should rest on the traditions and practices gleaned from the collective successes and failures of past culinary experience. Prevailing cultural preferences must also be taken into account. While preparing this volume, some recipe modifications were necessary to accommodate modern culinary practices and product availability. Dishes are designed to be served as "specials" or for special occasions. It is hoped that those who use this volume will continue to follow the long culinary tradition that combines experimentation and creativity with a healthy respect for the practices of untold generations of cooks who made these dishes possible.

ACKNOWLEDGMENTS

To express one's thanks to those who helped make this book possible would necessitate re-capping the historical events that shaped the cuisine described in this volume. The list would be extensive and would, in all fairness, have to include ship builders, map makers, navigators, provisioners, the noble houses of Spain and Portugal, native populations long gone yet ever present, and the intrepid men and women who sailed the uncharted waters to discover gold and, instead, uncovered a world of gastronomic riches. We owe them all a tremendous thanks. Their collective efforts at one specific time in our history initiated the great stream of edible products that ultimately encircled our globe. This availability of new products, served to inspire countless cooks, who, over the following centuries, experimented, refined and ultimately inspired so many of the food preparations found in our global kitchen.

That being said, I would like to also express my thanks to a number of my contemporaries, individuals who helped me in preparing this book. First, my thanks go to my wife, Margaret Bachelder, who served as my research assistant and who offered valuable editorial assistance, and to my daughter, Myriam Gelber, who served in a similar capacity. To my colleagues, Chef Charles Leonardo, C.E.C., assistant director of dining services at Northeastern University and President of The Epicurean Club of Boston, and Chef Mark Janicki, instructor of Culinary Arts in Boston, my everlasting gratitude for their willingness to share professional expertise and for their enthusiasm and interest in this project. A very special thanks to Chef Kurt Scheller, Executive Chef, Hotel Bristol in Warsaw, Poland for providing numerous professional sources for information throughout South America and the Caribbean. To Mr. Roberto Rodriguez of Panama, and Mr. Manny Spector whose roots lie in

Ecuador, two gentlemen whose enthusiasm for the culinary arts is truly inspirational, I give my sincere gratitude for providing me with both materials and personal insights about the cuisines of their respective countries. I would also like to acknowledge the assistance that I have received from the support staffs at the Embassies of Peru, Guatemala, Brazil, Chile, Columbia, and Mexico. And lastly, my thanks to Pamela Chirls and Anthony Calcara of Van Nostrand Reinhold for their patience and assistance in preparing these volumes.

INTRODUCTION

The International Kitchen comprises a collection of representative appetizers, soups, meat, fish and fowl entrées, and desserts from many countries around the world. The series is designed to provide students of the culinary arts, professional and amateur, with a handy reference to a number of interesting culinary specialities from diverse cultures. It is hoped that it will also afford them an opportunity to further their skills and knowledge, add variety to their menus, and bring joy to their friends and patrons.

Obviously, the number of recipes embraced by any single national or regional cuisine is enormous. And, if one multiplies this wealth of material by the number of countries represented in these volumes, the total number of potential recipes becomes staggering. To deal effectively with this abundant source of culinary ingenuity and invention, the recipes selected for inclusion had to meet four objectives:

1. have a strong association with a specific national cuisine;
2. use basic, raw ingredients that are readily available in the United States market;
3. be within the culinary realm of a broad spectrum of diners and therefore marketable;
4. reinforce basic culinary skills through the processes involved in their production.

The recipes are formulated in portions that are appropriate to the particular preparation. Items that should be produced in volume are designed, for the most part, for 10 to 12 portions that can then be expanded or reduced, if desired. Other dishes, primarily sauté items, which are best treated in individually prepared servings, are scaled for the single portion. If any components of these single-portion recipes can be prepared in advance (sauces, for example), directions are given to yield quantities sufficient for 10 to 12 servings.

The recipes are formatted in three columns. The first column is the ingredients, the second is the quantity, and the third is the method. This format was used because it presents each stage of the preparation in proper sequence. Furthermore, it relates the raw product to the operation necessary to process that phase of the recipe. This format eliminates going back and forth between a list of ingredients and the method of preparation. To assemble all ingredients prior to preparation, simply read down columns one and two. The following is an example.

SHRIMP "ESCABECHE"   *Peru*   Yield: 10–12 servings

Ingredient	Quantity	Method
Peanut oil	6 oz.	Heat the oil over high heat in a heavy skillet. Fry the shrimp quickly in small batches. Remove the shrimp as soon as they begin to turn pink, and place them in a deep glass or stainless-steel bowl. Do not overcook.
Shrimp, large, peeled, deveined, and tail end of shell left intact	4–5 lb. (21–25 count)	
Garlic cloves, peeled	6–8	Using the same pan, lower the heat to low. Add the garlic and chili peppers. Sauté slowly until the garlic turns golden (Do not let the garlic brown). Mash the cloves in the pan to extract their flavor, then discard both the garlic and peppers.
Chili pepper, red, dried	4	
Paprika, Spanish	1 tbsp.	In the same skillet, add the paprika. Cook for 20–30 seconds, stirring. Add the remaining ingredients, raise the heat to high, and bring to a boil. Lower the heat and simmer for 10–15 minutes. Let the liquid cool to warm, then pour over shrimp. When cool, remove bay leaf, cover, and refrigerate.
Vinegar, white wine	16 oz.	
White wine, dry	16 oz.	
Rosemary *or* thyme, fresh	4–5 sprigs or to taste	
Bay leaf	2	

Serve on a bed of lettuce and garnish with thick slices of corn on the cob, green pimiento-stuffed or black olives, chopped parsley, and white, soft cheese.

THE CUISINES OF LATIN AMERICA

To understand the cuisines of Latin America is to understand the impact of a grand encounter between two disparate cultures, which began when Columbus first sighted land in the New World in 1492. His discovery heralded many events that have helped to shape the modern world. It marked the beginning of a new empire and unimagined wealth for the Spanish Crown, and later, for other European nations; it signaled an end to the sovereignty of those native to the newly conquered lands and precipitated the decimation of their unique societies; it fueled the economic growth of the seafaring nations of Europe and their rapidly expanding colonial empires; and it gave birth to a new and vital culture that is now referred to as Latin American. Less than 20 years after Columbus's initial expedition, more than 10,000 Spaniards were living on the island of Hispaniola, and the produce of the New World was being exported in an ever-growing stream to enliven and enrich the European diet. Within 50 years, the New World's agricultural bounty had not only produced an unexpected, new form of wealth, but had also transformed the ways in which the Old World fed itself.

Since that time, human curiosity about and fascination with a diversified diet has continued. If Columbus's "discovery" is to be celebrated at all, it should be for its contribution to the exchange and proliferation of agricultural products between the New World and Europe. Previously unknown to the Europeans, these foods were enthusiastically received by Columbus's patrons in Spain, and, when subjected to the more advanced techniques of cultivation practiced in Europe at that time, flourished. Along with raw materials and other forms of wealth, the Spanish and, shortly thereafter, Portuguese merchant vessels carried cargoes of corn, tomatoes, beans, peppers, peanuts, white and sweet potatoes, vanilla, and chocolate back to Europe, along with some knowledge about their cultivation and use. Without these products, the sophisticated cuisines of modern Europe would have quite another flavor. Simultaneously, the diet of the peoples native to the Americas was forever changed. On their return to the new-found lands, the Europeans brought horses, cattle, chickens, pigs, rice, citrus fruits, and many herbs and spices. These European imports took root, flourished, and, when combined with the foods native to the Americas, produced new, unique cuisines: the cuisines of Latin America.

The initiators of these events, the crowned heads of Spain, combined military might, religious zeal, and mastery of the seas to exercise complete domination over the newly discovered lands in a relatively short period of time. While professing to bring civilization and religious enlightenment to the natives of the New World, they were engaged in pursuing their primary quest: to fill their coffers with gold and other treasures. The rapid convergence of the strengths and weaknesses of native and conquering cultures resulted in the redefinition of both, altering the lives of both conqueror and vanquished forever. While the drama of cultural convergence was to be replayed many times in other parts of the world, Latin America's experience remains unique. In no other place did the encounter between the Old and New Worlds occur so swiftly, so pervasively, and over as vast an area.

Long before Columbus's arrival, the indigenous inhabitants of Latin America had developed vibrant and complex civilizations with sophisticated concepts of art, architecture, science, and food production. While the remains of their ancient world continue to fascinate and impress us with their sophistication and complexity, the less tangible products of these civilizations are, of course, less evident. The peoples of the Andes, for instance, terraced their mountain slopes for the cultivation of crops, built irrigation systems, and domesticated animals for food, clothing, and labor. A healthy, prosperous people when first encountered by the Spaniards, it is certain that they had developed their own distinctive culinary practices. Today, the contemporary cuisines of Latin America strongly resonate with the ancient strains of their Indian heritage and are inextricably intertwined with flavors that are African, Spanish and Portuguese. To a lesser extent, they have also been touched by American, British, French, and other European influences. For the most part, these cuisines ignore the constraints of individual national boundaries and exploit the possibilities of the region's variegated terrain and diverse climates. Latin Americans have plumbed this rich heritage to produce cuisines that utilize the historic, indigenous food stocks in combination with European plant and livestock products that were adopted and developed into new varieties.

While much that is positive resulted from this great encounter between Europe and the New World, there was a price to pay; unfortunately, the cost was borne by the indigenous peoples. In an attempt to dispossess the native inhabitants of their lands and wealth, it has been estimated that the European conquerors caused the deaths of approximately 50 million people through warfare and disease. It was an act of genocide unparalleled until the World Wars of modern times. This decimation of the local inhabitants, in turn, created a labor shortage, affecting the newly developed sugarcane plantations and other economic enterprises that had been established by the conquering powers. The resulting need for labor was the primary factor in the importation of Africans and the institutionalization of slavery. Beginning in 1500 and continuing for about four centuries, some 10 million Africans, 2 million of whom died in transit, were sent to the Americas as slaves. Half of them landed in the Caribbean to work the sugar plantations, another third were sent to Brazil, and the remainder to other parts of the New World. The bitter legacy of this era is still with us today.

Columbus's expedition to the New World began the modern era of world trade, an activity that continues to dominate the relations between nations to this day. The benefits to mankind have been considerable. Through our global distribution networks, the exchange and transfer of food products has prevented famine and aided countless millions in times of distress. It has promoted the development of new, hardier food crops, encouraged the development of commerce, and promoted cultural exchange between geographically separated peoples, sparking the emergence of a more discriminating and multicultural international consumer with expanded tastes, preferences, and a heightened curiosity about the production, procedures, and processes of food handling worldwide.

For the past 500 years, since that first "international" exchange of foods took place in the Caribbean, the flow of foods from one country to another has continued unabated, steadily increasing as methods of transport have become more sophisticated. Thus, the explorations of the New World by the Europeans resulted not only in great territorial conquests accompanied by material wealth, but also in access to an expanded and exciting menu of foodstuffs. The creative use of this edible treasure has had a profound effect on the world's diet and nutrition. The great cuisines of Europe and, to some extent, of Asia, owe much to the native products of the Americas, as the food crops native to Latin America have become an integral part of the world's daily diet. The introduction of the foods of Europe into Latin America expanded the repertoire of native dishes, creating a cuisine unique to the world.

ABOUT CHILI PEPPERS

One of Latin America's most distinctive gifts to the culinary world, chili peppers, members of the genus *Capsicum*, are native to Central and South America. Classified among the nightshade family, which contains approximately 2,000 species, chili peppers are related botanically to the tomato, tamarillo, potato, and tobacco. It is believed that chili peppers have been grown by humans since 7000 B.C., making them among the oldest known cultivated plants. They were widely consumed throughout Mexico, the Caribbean, and Central and South America before the arrival of Columbus. On his return to Spain, Columbus brought chili peppers, along with other plant specimens from the Caribbean, which had never before been seen outside of the Americas. It took only 50 years for chili peppers to be cultivated widely throughout Europe. Used primarily as a flavoring agent, chili peppers have also been employed for medicinal purposes. Now cultivated virtually everywhere, chili peppers are considered by some to be one of the American continent's most universally accepted contributions to the kitchens of the world, playing an important role in the culinary preparations of the divergent cooking styles of Asia, Africa, Latin America, the Mediterranean, and, to a lesser extent, the United States and Europe. It is estimated that more than 200 varieties are grown throughout the world.

The flavors and heat properties of chili peppers can vary enormously from one variety to another. Not all chilies possess a fiery nature. Poblanos, for example, have very thick flesh and a relatively mild flavor, making them ideal for stuffing. Chili peppers vary in size and can be found as small as one-fourth inch, or as long as 8 to 10 inches. While it is generally believed that smaller chilies are hotter than larger ones, this is not necessarily true. The degree of heat can vary greatly even among chilies of the same type. In addition to their fiery personalities, chilies of different types also have distinctive flavors. Capsaicin, the principle substance responsible for the unique character of the chili pepper, is found on the interior ribs of the chili pods. When cut or chopped, this reddish, oily substance will impart the "heat" to the nearby seeds as well. For this reason, many recipes calling for chilies recommend the removal of the ribs and seeds before using them. Another way to control the flavoring strength of the chili pepper is to gently sauté the whole pods in oil, then use the oil to flavor the dish. Still another method is to immerse the whole chili pod in simmering liquid and remove it when the desired degree of flavor has been imparted to the liquid.

Chili peppers are used both fresh and dried, and vary in color from a deep, black green to vivid oranges and reds. The colors are indicative of the stage in the ripening cycle and have nothing to do with degree of hotness. When fresh chilies are minced, the amount added to the recipe can be carefully controlled. Chilies may be peeled by charring the skins directly over a flame or on a hot griddle, then covering them for 5 to 10 minutes to let the skin loosen. Dried chilies are often soaked in water or vinegar, then pureed, shredded, or ground before using. Chilies may also be purchased pickled. Chipotle chilies, which are ripe jalapeños that have been dried and smoked, may be purchased canned, either in vinegar or adobo sauce.

Great care should be taken when working with chili peppers as capsaicin can cause severe irritation. If some of this heat-producing substance is transferred accidentally from the hands to the eyes, nose, or other sensitive areas of the body, painful burning can result. For this reason, chilies should never be handled carelessly. When processing large quantities, the use of rubber gloves is suggested. Chili peppers should be eaten with moderation. When consumed in small quantities, they stimulate gastric secretions; if used in excess, they can cause severe internal inflammation.

Chili peppers enhance the foods of many cultures. They are used by some in subtle ways to enrich flavors, while others value the heat they impart above all else.

Largely unused outside of the southwestern regions of the United States until recently, chili peppers are now beginning to appear more frequently in markets throughout the country as are a wide variety of sauces and other condiments made from chili peppers. The large influx of people from Asia and Latin America into the United States has created a demand for these products and their use is gradually becoming a part of our national diet as we learn to appreciate their piquant qualities.

REGIONAL FLAVORINGS

ACHIOTE OIL   *Latin America*   Yield: 8 oz.

Achiote (annatto) seeds	2 oz.
Olive oil	8 oz.

Soak the seeds in the oil for 30–40 minutes. Bring to a simmer over low heat, stirring frequently. The exact cooking time will vary from 1–3 minutes, depending on the freshness of the seeds. The oil will become a deep orange-red in color. If the oil begins to lighten as you cook it, remove it from the heat immediately. Let cool and strain through several layers of cheesecloth. Place in a well-sealed container and store in the refrigerator.

Achiote oil is used primarily as a coloring agent. It imparts a bright yellow color to foods as well as a mild, distinctive flavor. Use seeds that have a bright reddish brown color for optimum results. Crumpled dried chili pepper and bay leaf may be added during cooking for other flavoring possibilities. Strain and discard any added ingredients after the oil has cooled.

ACHIOTE PASTE   *Mexico*   Yield: approximately 10 oz.

Achiote seeds	8 oz.

In a spice or coffee grinder, grind the seeds to a powder a small amount at a time. If necessary, remove and re-grind any large particles.

Oregano	4 tsp.
Clove	4 tsp.
Cumin seed	3 tsp.
Cinnamon	2 tsp.
Coriander	2 tsp.
Salt	2 tsp.
Garlic, minced*	

Grind the herbs and seasonings and blend with the ground achiote seeds.

(Continued)

* Minced garlic is used generously in combination with this spice and herb mixture and may be added to the above ingredients. If used in small quantities and stored, add garlic to taste just prior to using.

Water *or* cider vinegar	as needed

Gradually add small amounts of water or cider vinegar to the ground herb mixture and mix well to create a stiff paste. Place in a well-sealed container and store in the refrigerator.

Used as a coloring and flavoring agent, achiote seeds may also be ground into a paste with herbs other than those listed. Proportions as well as ingredients can vary significantly, depending on regional taste preferences. A popular seasoning in the Yucatan region of Mexico, it is used with fish, fowl, grilled meats, roasts, and tamales.

BARBADOS RUB

Yield: approximately 2 lb.

Onion, peeled and quartered	2 lb.
Garlic, peeled	6 cloves
Jalapeño peppers roasted, peeled, seeds and veins removed	2
Scallions	2–3
Oregano	1 tbsp.
Cloves, ground	1 tsp.
Salt and black pepper	to taste
Lime juice, fresh	2–3 tbsp.

In a food processor fitted with a steel blade, puree all ingredients until smooth. Refrigerate.

Rub a thin layer of this seasoning mix on fish, poultry, or meat an hour or two before grilling, broiling, or roasting.

UNDILUTED OR "THICK" COCONUT MILK   *Latin America*

Yield: approximately 1 qt.

Coconuts	8

To select coconuts that are suitable, first check to see if the "eyes" at the top are intact, then shake each coconut to determine that it contains a generous amount of liquid. Pierce the eyes with a clean ice pick and drain the water through a fine sieve or several layers of cheesecloth. Taste the liquid from each of the coconuts separately to determine whether its liquid is rancid. The coconut's liquid should taste slightly sweet. If rancid, discard both the liquid and the coconut. Reserve the liquid from the fresh coconuts and set aside.

Place the coconuts in a 400 degree F oven for 15 minutes. When cool enough to handle, wrap each coconut in a towel and crack open with a mallet. Remove the outer shell, then peel away the brown skin adhering to the coconut meat. Wash the meat, then grate or place the meat in a food processor. Using the pulsing action, puree the meat to a fine, but not overly fine, consistency. Place the coconut meat in a muslin bag with the reserved coconut liquid and squeeze out as much of the liquid as possible. Reserve for cooking.

Reserve the coconut meat to make diluted or "thin" coconut milk.

DILUTED OR "THIN" COCONUT MILK

Yield: approximately 3 qt.

Coconut pulp, reserved	
Water, boiling	3 qt.

Pour boiling water over the coconut pulp and let sit for 45 minutes. Squeeze through a muslin cloth. Discard the pulp and reserve the liquid for other recipes.

COCONUT MILK—VERSION 3

Yield: 1 qt.

Coconut, whole	one, 26–30 oz.

Follow the above procedures to select and remove meat from the coconut. Reserve the coconut liquid and add enough cold water to make up 1 qt. Peel, then cut coconut meat into 1-inch squares. Place the coconut in the bowl of a food processor fitted with a steel blade and chop fine. Gradually add the coconut water to the chopped coconut. Pour through a metal sieve; using a large spoon, press pulp to extract as much liquid as possible.

ADOBO   *Mexico*

Yield: approximately ½ lb.

Ancho chilies	8 oz.

Slit open the chilies and remove the seeds. Place chilies in a glass or stainless steel container and cover with boiling water. Let steep for 1 hour. Drain, then remove any membrane, remaining seeds, or stems. Using a spoon or the back of a paring knife, scrape the pulp from the skins. Discard the skins. Place the pulp into the bowl of a food processor fitted with a steel blade.

Vinegar	4 oz.
Olive oil	2 oz.
Garlic, minced	2 tbsp.
Salt	2 – 3 tsp.
Oregano	2 tsp.
Thyme	1 tsp.
Cumin, ground	½ tsp.
Black pepper	½ tsp.
Cinnamon	½ tsp.

Add the vinegar, oil, garlic, herbs, and seasonings to the chili pulp and blend using the pulse action.

Refrigerate until needed or freeze for future use. Adobo paste is used as a flavoring for chicken and pork dishes.

JERK MARINADE — VERSION 1   *Jamaica*

Yield: approximately 2¼ lb.

Onion, large dice	2 lb.
Scallions, white and green parts	6
Vinegar, white	2 oz.
Corn oil	2 oz.
Hot pepper flakes	2 – 3 tsp. or to taste
Sugar	2 tbsp.

Place all ingredients in the bowl of a food processor fitted with a steel blade. Puree until very smooth. Place in a jar with a tight-fitting lid and refrigerate until needed.

Thyme	1 tbsp.
Allspice, ground	1 tbsp.
Salt	2 tsp.
Black pepper	2 tsp.

Use to marinate chicken parts, thin cuts of pork, beef, or fish for broiling.

JERK MARINADE — VERSION 2   *Jamaica*

Yield: marinade for 10 – 12 lb of product

Onions	2 ½ lb.
Peppers, fresh hot. Scotch Bonnet or Jalapenos	1 lb.
Ginger root	4 oz.
Pepper, black	3 oz.
Thyme	2 oz.
Allspice, ground	2 oz.
Vinegar, white wine	1 pint
Soy Sauce, dark	1 pint
Sesame oil, toasted	2 oz.

Peel and quarter onions. Remove stem ends of peppers. Slice them in half and remove the seeds. Peel and slice the ginger root. Place these ingredients into the bowl of a food processor fitted with the steel blade and process to a smooth puree.

Add these ingredients to the mixture in the bowl of the processor and pulse until thoroughly blended. Transfer contents to a glass or stainless steel mixing bowl.

Add these ingredients and mix well.

Use to marinate whole chickens, thick cuts of pork, beef, or whole fish for baking or roasting.

SOFRITO — VERSION 1   *Cuba*

Yield: approximately 1 qt.

Achiote oil (see recipe earlier in this section)	16 oz.
Onion, chopped	1½ lb.
Green bell pepper, seeded, ribs removed, chopped	1 lb.

Place all ingredients in the bowl of a food processor fitted with a steel blade and puree until smooth. Transfer the mixture to a heavy-bottomed saucepan. Simmer, covered, over low heat, for 20 – 25 minutes. Let cool and refrigerate in a tightly covered container.

(Continued)

Ham, cured, chopped	1 lb.
Tomatoes, chopped	1 lb.
Green chilies, mild, chopped	3
Cilantro leaves	1 bunch
Garlic, minced	2 tbsp.
Oregano, dried	2 tsp.
Salt	1 tsp.

SOFRITO — VERSION 2
Puerto Rico

Yield: approximately 3¼ lb.

Slab bacon, small dice	½ lb.	Fry bacon until crisp. Remove from rendered fat and reserve. Add achiote seeds to bacon fat and cook over medium heat until color has been released. Remove seeds and discard them.
Achiote seeds	3 tbsp.	

Onion, chopped	1½ lb.	Add the onion, green pepper, and garlic to the pan and sauté over low heat until soft. Do not allow to brown.
Green pepper, chopped	1 lb.	
Garlic, peeled and chopped	1 head	

Tomato, peeled and chopped	2 lb.	Add the tomato, herbs, and reserved cooked bacon and cook over low heat for 30–40 minutes. Adjust seasoning as needed. Let cool; cover, then refrigerate in a glass container until needed.
Cilantro leaves, fresh, chopped	4 tbsp.	
Oregano, dried	1 tbsp.	
Salt and black pepper	to taste	

Salsas, Condiments, and Dressings

LIME SALAD DRESSING   *Mexico*

Yield: approximately 1 qt.

Lime zest	2 limes
Serrano chilies, seeded and chopped	2
Garlic, chopped	1 tbsp.

Use very fresh limes with tender skins. Remove skin in strips and blanche in boiling water for 30 seconds. Place in the bowl of a food processor along with the chilies and garlic and chop fine using a steel blade.

Vegetable oil	24 oz.
Lime juice, fresh squeezed	8 oz.
Feta cheese	4 oz.
Coriander leaves, fresh, chopped	6 tbsp.
Salt and white pepper	to taste

Add oil, lime juice, feta, and coriander and process until smooth. Add salt and pepper to taste and mix, using the pulse action, until well blended. Keep refrigerated until needed.

PICKLED ONIONS   *Mexico*

Yield: 2 lb.

Red onions, peeled and sliced thin	2 lb.

Place onions in enough cold water to cover and bring to a boil. Cook for 1–2 minutes, then remove from heat. With a slotted spoon, place the onions in ice water. Reserve the cooking liquid.

Oregano	1 tbsp.
Garlic, chopped	1 tbsp.
Peppercorns, black, crushed	1 tsp.
Cumin seeds	1 tsp.
Salt	1 tsp.

Add the garlic, herbs, and seasonings to the reserved cooking liquid and simmer until reduced by half. Let cool.

(Continued)

Cider vinegar	as needed

Drain the onions and, in a glass or stainless-steel bowl, combine with the cooking liquid. Add enough vinegar to bring the level of liquid just to the top of the onions. Mix well and refrigerate until needed.

PAPAYA CHUTNEY *Cuba*

Yield: approximately 3 lb.

Papaya, ripe, peeled and cubed	3
Water	12 oz.
Onion, large dice	1 lb.
Pepper, red bell, small dice	8 oz.
Sugar	8 oz.
Cider vinegar	6 oz.
Raisins	4 oz.
Ginger root, minced	2 tsp.
Clove, ground	1 tsp.
Cinnamon, ground	½ tsp.
Chili pepper, dried	1
Salt	1 tsp.

Combine all ingredients in a stainless-steel saucepan and bring to a boil over medium heat. Lower heat and simmer for 30–40 minutes, stirring occasionally. When done, remove the chili pepper and discard. Let cool to room temperature before serving.

AVOCADO DRESSING *Mexico*

Yield: 1 qt.

Avocado pulp	1 lb.
Vegetable oil	10 oz.
Lime juice, fresh squeezed	3 oz.
Cider vinegar	2 oz.
Garlic, crushed	2 tsp.
Coriander leaves, fresh, chopped	6 tbsp.

Place the avocado, oil, lime juice, vinegar, garlic, and coriander in the bowl of a food processor and puree until very smooth.

Egg yolks	2
Heavy cream	3 oz.
Tabasco sauce	to taste
Salt and white pepper	to taste
Scallions, finely sliced, white and tender green parts	2

In a separate mixing bowl, thoroughly beat the egg yolks and heavy cream with a wire whisk. Add the avocado mixture a little at a time to achieve a light, smooth, creamy texture. Add tabasco sauce, salt and pepper to taste. Fold in scallions and keep refrigerated until needed.

TOMATILLO-JALAPEÑO SALSA   *Mexico*

Yield: approximately 3 lb.

Tomatillos, husks removed and washed	3 lb.
Jalapeños, seeded	3
Coriander leaves, fresh, chopped	10 sprigs
Onion, chopped	½ lb.
Garlic, chopped	3 tsp.
Salt	1 tsp.

Simmer tomatillos for 5–6 minutes in lightly salted water. Drain, then place in the bowl of a food processor along with the jalapeños, coriander, onion, garlic, and salt. Process using the pulse action until well combined but not too smooth. Reserve.

Vegetable oil or lard	1–2 oz.
Stock, beef *or* chicken*	1 pt.
Salt	to taste

In a heavy skillet large enough to hold the tomatillo mixture, heat the oil over medium to high heat. When the oil is hot but still below the smoking point, add the reserved tomatillo mixture and cook, stirring, for 5 minutes. Add the stock and bring to a boil. Reduce heat and simmer for 20 minutes or until the sauce is thick enough to coat the back of a spoon. Adjust for salt, if needed. Let cool, then refrigerate.

This salsa can be made well in advance. It keeps well when covered and refrigerated.

*Use beef stock with meat entrées; chicken stock with poultry.

TOMATILLO-CHIPOTLES
SALSA   *Mexico*

Yield: approximately 2 lb.

Tomatillos, husks removed and washed	2 lb.
Garlic, unpeeled, cloves separated	1 large bulb
Vegetable oil	as needed

In a small roasting pan, lightly coat the tomatillos and garlic cloves with oil. Place both in a 400 degree F oven until the garlic softens. Let cool. Peel the garlic and place it along with the tomatillos, into the bowl of a food processor fitted with a steel blade.

Chipotle chilies, canned	10 or to taste
Water	as needed

Add the chipotles and puree until smooth. Add a small amount of water or the liquid in which the chilies were packed to lighten the texture or alter the flavor to taste.

SWEET RED PEPPER
SAUCE   *Cuba*

Yield: approximately 3¼ lb.

Red bell peppers, seeded, halved	3 lb.

Place the peppers on an oiled sheet pan and bake at 450 degrees F until the skins char. Remove from oven and cover with a towel. When cool enough to handle, peel and chop. Reserve.

Olive oil	4 oz.
Tomatoes, peeled and chopped	1½ lb.
Tomato paste	1 tbsp.
Paprika, Spanish	2 tsp.
Oregano	2 tsp.
Sugar	2 tsp.
Cayenne	½ tsp. or to taste
Salt and black pepper	to taste

Heat the oil in a heavy saucepan over medium heat. Cook the tomatoes and the tomato paste, stirring, for 3–4 minutes. Lower heat and add the seasonings and reserved peppers. Simmer until the sauce has thickened.

Vinegar, white	to taste

Add vinegar; adjust seasoning with salt and pepper, if needed.

Served as a sauce for black beans, or meat or fish entrées.

SALSA CRUDA—VERSION
1   *Mexico*

Yield: approximately 3 lb.

Tomatoes, ripe, peeled, seeded, and chopped fine	3 lb.
Chilies, long, green, seeded and chopped fine	3
Onion, diced	½ lb.
Garlic, minced	1 tsp.
Cilantro leaves, fresh, chopped	4 tbsp.

Combine all ingredients. A better texture is obtained if the ingredients are chopped with a knife, or, if using a food processor, by utilizing the pulse action.

This salsa should be used within several hours of preparation.

SALSA CRUDA—VERSION
2   *South America*

Yield: approximately 3½ lb.

Cucumbers, peeled, seeded, and chopped fine	2 lb.
Tomatoes, peeled, seeded, and chopped	6 oz.
Red bell pepper, seeded, deveined, and chopped	6 oz.
Celery, strings removed and chopped	4 oz.
Scallions, white and green parts, chopped	6
Jalapeños, seeded and minced	2

In a stainless steel or glass bowl, combine the chopped vegetables.

(Continued)

Olive oil	4 oz.
Lime *or* lemon juice, fresh squeezed	3 oz.
Cilantro leaves, chopped	6 tbsp.
Ginger root, chopped	1 tbsp. or to taste
Salt	2 tsp. or to taste

Combine the remaining ingredients, mix well, and add to the other ingredients. Mix again and serve as fresh as possible.

SALSA VERDE   *Mexico*

Yield: approximately 3 lb.

Tomatillos, husks removed and washed	3 lb.
Serrano chilies, stem ends removed	8–10 or to taste
Water	as needed

Place tomatillos and fresh chilies in a sauce pan with enough water to cover. Bring to a boil, then lower heat and simmer until the tomatillos are soft. Cooking time will vary depending on ripeness of tomatillos. When done, strain, reserving the cooking water. Place the tomatillos and chilies in the bowl of a food processor fitted with a steel blade.

Cilantro leaves	5–6 sprigs
Garlic, minced	1 tbsp.
Oil, corn	3 oz.
Salt	to taste
Cooking water	as needed

Add the cilantro, garlic, corn oil and salt. Use the pulse action of the processor to create a coarse textured mixture. Add some of the cooking water to create desired consistency.

PUREED JALAPEÑO SALSA   *Mexico*

Yield: approximately 1 lb.

Jalapeños	12 oz.
Water	as needed

Place jalapeños in a small saucepan and add water to cover. Bring to a boil, then lower heat and simmer until the peppers become soft. Drain the peppers; reserve the cooking liquid and set aside. When cool enough to handle, slit the peppers and remove the stems and seeds. Place in the bowl of a food processor or blender equipped with a steel blade.

Onion, grated	8 oz.
Cider vinegar	2 oz.
Salt	to taste
Sugar	to taste

Add the remaining ingredients to the peppers and process to a smooth puree. If a thinner consistency is desired, add some of the cooking liquid.

Serve in small amounts over grilled meats and poultry.

ORANGE-LIME SALSA   *Cuba*

Yield: approximately 2½ lb.

Tomatoes, ripe, peeled, seeded, and chopped	2½ lb.
Onion, minced	12 oz.
Jalapeños, seeded, ribs removed, and minced	3 or to taste
Orange juice, fresh squeezed	6 oz.
Lime juice, fresh squeezed	2 oz.
Orange rind, grated	2 tsp.
Salt and black pepper	to taste

Combine all ingredients, mix well, and refrigerate until needed. Best when served fresh.

Use as a condiment for grilled meats.

JALAPEÑO SALSA   *Mexico*

Yield: approximately 2¼ lb.

Oil, olive *or* corn	2 oz.
Onion, chopped	8 oz.
Jalapeños, seeded and minced	4–5
Garlic, minced	2 tsp.

In a heavy-bottomed saucepan, heat the oil over low to medium heat and sauté the onions until soft but not brown. Add the jalapeños and garlic and continue to cook over low heat for another minute.

(Continued)

Tomatoes, peeled, seeded, and coarsely chopped	2 lb.	Prepare tomatoes, then check their weight. Add the tomatoes, vinegar, and salt and pepper, and bring to a boil. Lower heat immediately, then simmer for 5 minutes. Remove salsa from heat and let cool to room temperature.
Vinegar, red wine	2 oz.	
Salt and black pepper	to taste	

Cilantro leaves, fresh chopped	10–12 sprigs or to taste	When cool, add the chopped cilantro. Refrigerate until needed.

SERRANO SALSA   *Mexico*

Yield: approximately 2 lb.

Tomatoes, large, firm	2½ lb.	Cut tomatoes in half and remove the inedible stem ends. Place the tomatoes skin side down over hot coals or on a grill. When skins begin to char, turn tomatoes to the other side and repeat the process. When done, place tomatoes in the bowl of a food processor equipped with a steel blade.

Serranos *or* jalapeños	2–4 to taste	Split the peppers and remove the seeds. Grill over hot coals or on a grill, turning once, until they begin to char. When done, add to the grilled tomatoes.

Vinegar, red wine	1–2 oz.	Add the vinegar and salt, and, using the pulse action, process briefly to obtain a slightly chunky texture.
Salt	to taste	

GREEN MANGO CHUTNEY   *Martinique*

Yield: approximately 2 lb.

Mangoes, green	5

Peel the mangoes by scoring the skin lengthwise on either of the long seed, then pare the skin between these vertical cuts. Cut the flesh from the seed on both sides. Score the flesh vertically and horizontally, pressing the skin inward so that the scored sections separate. Slice off the cubed sections. (For every 1 lb. of unpeeled, unpitted fruit, the usable yield is about 6 oz.) Place the mango in the bowl of a food processor fitted with a steel blade.

Onion, grated	4 oz.
Pepper, red bell, seeded	1
Jalapeño, seeded and minced *or* cayenne	to taste
Parsley, flat leaf, chopped	4 tbsp.
Peanut oil	2 oz.
Salt and black pepper	to taste

Add the remaining ingredients and puree until very smooth.

Serve with fish or hot or cold meat entrées.

CHIMICHURRI   *Argentina*

Yield: approximately 2 lb.

Olive oil	16 oz.
Vinegar	6 oz.

Using a wire whisk, combine the oil and vinegar. Adjust for a good balance between the two.

(Continued)

West Lafayette Public Library
West Lafayette, Indiana

Onions, minced	1 lb.
Garlic, minced	2 tsp.
Oregano, dried	2 tsp.
Cayenne pepper	½ tsp. or to taste
Parsley *or* cilantro leaves (or a combination), fresh, chopped	15 sprigs
Salt	2 tsp. or to taste
Black pepper, coarse ground	2 tsp. or to taste

Add the remaining ingredients and mix well. Let stand for several hours at room temperature before serving.

This parsley sauce is used as a condiment for roasted and grilled meats.

GUACAMOLE — VERSION 1   *Mexico*

Yield: approximately 2 lb.

Tomato, peeled and seeded	8 oz.
Onion, diced	4 oz.
Jalapeño, seeded and chopped fine	2 tsp. or to taste
Garlic, minced	1 tsp.
Lime juice	2 oz. or to taste
Cilantro leaves, fresh, chopped	3 tbsp.

Place the tomato, onion, jalapeño, garlic, lime juice, and cilantro into the bowl of a food processor, and, using a steel blade, puree to a fine consistency.

Avocado pulp	1½ lb.
Cilantro leaves, fresh, chopped	as needed

Add the avocado pulp and, using the pulsing action sparingly, mix ingredients thoroughly. The texture should be slightly lumpy. Sprinkle with chopped, fresh cilantro leaves.

Guacamole may be served as a salad, as a garnish, or as a dip. The number of portions will vary according to use. Since guacamole is best when served fresh, it should not be made far in advance of serving time.

GUACAMOLE—VERSION
2   *Mexico*

Yield: approximately 2 lb.

Onion, minced	4 oz.
Cilantro leaves, chopped fine	4 tbsp.
Serrano chilies, seeded and chopped fine	3 or to taste
Salt	½ tsp.

Place the onion, cilantro, serranos, and salt into the bowl of a food processor fitted with a steel blade and chop as fine as possible.

Tomatillos	8 oz.

Remove the thin, paperlike husks from the tomatillos and wash. Place 2–3 inches from broiler flame and broil until skins begin to char. Add the tomatillos to the onion/serrano mixture and puree until smooth.

Avocado pulp	1½ lb.
Onion, chopped	as needed
Cilantro leaves, chopped	as needed

In a clean mixing bowl, mash the onion/serrano mixture with the avocado. The texture should be slightly lumpy. If used as a dip, place in a chilled bowl and garnish with chopped onion and cilantro.

GUACAMOLE—VERSION
3   *Mexico*

Yield: approximately 2 lb.

Avocado pulp	1½ lb.
Lime *or* lemon juice, fresh squeezed	3 oz.
Sour cream	6 oz.
Onion, grated	2 tbsp.
Garlic, crushed	1 tsp.
Jalapeños, seeded, ribs removed, and minced (optional)	2 tsp.
Cilantro leaves, chopped	4 tbsp.

Cut the avocados in half and remove and discard pits. Scoop out the pulp and mash coarsely with a fork. Add the remaining ingredients and mix well.

LIGHT DISHES AND APPETIZERS

EMPANADAS DOUGH
Latin America

Yield: approximately 40 small empanadas

Flour, all-purpose, sifted	1 lb.
Salt	½ tsp.
Butter, chilled, cut in small dice	8 oz.
Egg yolks	3
Cider vinegar	2 tbsp.
Water, iced	5 – 8 tbsp. or as needed

Assembly:
Filling of choice (see following recipes)

Egg and water, beaten	1 egg/2 tbsp. water

Place the flour, salt, and butter in the bowl of a food processor and pulse until the mixture has the texture of coarse meal. Add the egg yolks, vinegar, and water. Process until the dough forms a firm ball. Divide the dough in two and shape into balls, then flatten into discs. Wrap in plastic and refrigerate for an hour or more before using.

Turn out the dough on a lightly floured surface and roll thin. Cut into 4-inch circles and place 1 tablespoon of filling in the center of each circle. Using a pastry brush, lightly moisten the circumference with the beaten egg and water, then fold over to create a half-moon shape. Pinch edges together to seal. Or, cut the dough into 4-inch squares, fill, then fold to make a triangular shape. Seal edges in a similar manner. Create an attractive fluted pattern along the edge using the tines of a fork, spoon tip, or your fingers. For larger-sized portions, cut circles 7 – 9 inches in diameter and use proportionally more filling. Seal the edges in a similar manner, turn back the sealed edge approximately ¼ inch to double its thickness, then decorate the edge.

Utilize all scraps of dough by kneading them together and rolling out once again. Before baking, prick the tops of the empanadas 2 – 3 times with a sharp-tined fork. Brush with the beaten egg and water to glaze and place on a lightly oiled sheet pan lined with parchment

(Continued)

paper. Bake in a 375 – 400 degree F oven 20 – 25 minutes or until golden brown. Empanadas may also be deep-fried in oil heated to a temperature of 375 degrees F.

EMPANADAS FILLINGS   *Latin America*

Yield: approximately 40 small empanadas

Beef:

Beef, chuck	8 oz.
Salt	½ tsp.
Peppercorns, black	½ tsp.

Cut beef into 1½-inch cubes and place in a small saucepan with just enough water to cover. Bring to a boil, skim, cover, then lower heat to a simmer. Add the salt and peppercorns. Cook until meat is very tender. Let meat cool in the broth, then shred the meat into small pieces using your fingers or in a food processor with a plastic blade. Strain and reserve the broth and set aside.

Oil *or* lard	1 tbsp.
Onion, small dice	4 oz.
Garlic, minced	1 tsp.
Cumin	1 tsp.
Oregano	1 tsp.

Heat the oil in a large skillet and sauté the onion and garlic until soft. Add the cumin and oregano and cook for another minute or two. Add the shredded meat and continue to sauté until the meat begins to brown slightly.

Tomatoes, peeled and pureed	1 lb.
Salt and black pepper	to taste
Tabasco sauce	to taste

Add tomatoes and simmer for 30 – 40 minutes. If mixture becomes too dry add some of the reserved beef broth. Season with salt, pepper, and tabasco sauce.

Variation: Beef Filling:

Apple, peeled and chopped	6 oz.
Raisins	2 oz.
Cinnamon, ground	to taste
Clove, ground	to taste
Salt and black pepper	to taste

Add these ingredients along with the tomatoes in Step 3. Simmer for 30 – 40 minutes. Use the reserved beef broth to keep the mixture moist but not too wet. Adjust seasoning to taste.

Chicken:

Chicken breast	12 oz.
Salt	½ tsp.
Peppercorns, black	½ tsp.

Place the chicken in a small saucepan with just enough water to cover. Bring to a boil, skim, add salt and peppercorns, then lower heat and simmer for 8 – 10 minutes or until the chicken is done. When cool enough to handle, shred the chicken into small pieces using your fingers or in a food processor with a plastic blade. Strain and reserve the broth.

Oil	1 tbsp.
Onion, small dice	4 oz.
Garlic, minced	2 tsp.
Tomatillos, husks removed and washed, then chopped fine	8 oz.
Cilantro, fresh, chopped	5 sprigs or to taste
Salt and black pepper	to taste

In a small, heavy skillet, heat the oil and sauté the onions until soft. Add the garlic and continue to cook for another minute. Add the tomatillos and enough of the reserved chicken broth to make a moist mixture. Simmer for 15 – 20 minutes or until most of the liquid has evaporated. Add the shredded chicken and cilantro and mix well. Add salt and pepper.

Fresh Fish:

Olive oil	1 tbsp.
Onion, small dice	4 oz.
Garlic, minced	1 tsp.
Poblano chilies, fresh, roasted, peeled, seeded, ribs removed, then chopped	3

Heat the oil in a skillet large enough to hold the fish. Over low heat, sauté the onions, garlic, and poblano chilies until soft.

Tomatoes, peeled and chopped	1 lb.
Salt and black pepper	to taste

Add the tomatoes and simmer for 15 minutes, or until most of the liquid has evaporated. Add salt and pepper.

Fish fillets (any firm-fleshed white fish cut into 1½-inch pieces)	8 oz.

Add the fish and cover the pan. Cook over medium heat until the fish flakes easily. Break the pieces of fish apart with a fork and blend with the other ingredients in the pan.

Salt Cod:

Salt cod	1 lb.

Soak the cod for 24 hours, changing the water several times. When ready to cook, place the fish in a saucepan and add water to cover. Bring to a boil, then lower the heat and simmer for 10–15 minutes, or until the fish flakes easily. Remove the fish from water and trim. Use only the white portions of the fish. Break the fish into small flakes and reserve.

Olive oil	3 oz.
Scallions, tender green and white parts, chopped	10–12
Garlic, minced	1 tbsp.
Serranos *or* jalapeños, seeded, ribs removed, and minced	4

In a heavy skillet, heat the oil over medium heat and sauté the scallions until soft. Add the garlic and chilies and sauté over low heat for 2–3 minutes.

Tomatoes, peeled, seeded, and chopped	1 lb.

Add the reserved cod and the tomatoes to the pan and cook long enough to evaporate any liquids.

Cilantro leaves, fresh, chopped fine	4 tbsp.

Add the cilantro and mix well.

Vegetable:

Olive oil	3 tbsp.
Onion, diced	1 lb.

In a large skillet, heat the oil over medium heat and sauté the onions until they begin to color slightly.

Tomatoes, peeled, seeded, and chopped fine	1½ lb.
Serranos *or* jalapeños, seeded, ribs removed, and minced	2
Ginger root, peeled and minced	1 tbsp.
Cumin, ground	1 tbsp.
Garlic, minced	2 tsp.
Curry powder	1 tsp.
Cinnamon	½ tsp.

Add tomatoes, chilies, ginger root, cumin, garlic, curry powder, and cinnamon and simmer for 5–6 minutes, stirring occasionally.

Potatoes, boiled and riced or mashed	1 lb.
Red bell pepper, diced fine	4 oz.
Peas, fresh or frozen	2 oz.
Parsley leaves, chopped	6 tbsp.
Water	6 oz.
Salt and white pepper	to taste

Add the potatoes and mix well. Then add the remaining ingredients and simmer, covered, for 5 minutes. Remove lid and adjust seasonings to taste. Simmer for 2–3 minutes more or until all of the liquid has evaporated.

Let all filling mixtures cool before assembling empanadas.

MACKEREL MARINATED IN LIME   *Mexico*

Yield: 10–12 servings

Mackerel fillet	2¼ lb.
Lime juice, fresh squeezed	16 oz.

Check fillets to ensure that all bones have been removed. Cut fish into ½-inch or smaller cubes. Place fish into a glass or stainless-steel bowl and mix thoroughly with the lime juice. Cover and marinate in the refrigerator for at least 6 hours. If the fish still has a raw look, let it marinate a bit longer before proceeding to the next step.

Tomato, peeled, seeded, and chopped fine; juice reserved	12 oz.
Onion, red, small dice	6 oz.
Green olives, pitted and chopped	30
Jalapeños, seeded, ribs removed, and minced	2 or to taste
Cilantro leaves, fresh, chopped fine	4 tbsp.
Oregano, dried	2 tsp.
Olive oil	2 oz.
Salt	1 tsp.
Sugar	1 tsp.
Tomato juice	as needed

Mix the remaining ingredients together. Place the fish in a colander to drain, then combine with tomato/olive mixture. Add the reserved, fresh tomato juice. If more liquid is desired, add a small amount of canned tomato juice.

Serve as an appetizer in small, chilled bowls garnished with cubes of avocado that have been tossed in fresh lime juice. If served as a luncheon entrée, garnish with an additional array of garden vegetables.

SHELLFISH SEVICHE   *Mexico*   Yield: 10–12 servings

Shrimp, peeled, deveined, and butterflied	1 lb.	In a glass or stainless-steel container, toss the shrimp in the lime or lemon juice. Cover and refrigerate overnight, mixing occasionally.
Lime or lemon juice, fresh squeezed	12 oz.	

Tomato, peeled, seeded, and chopped	2 lb.	Combine the tomato, onion, cilantro, and jalapeño and add to the shrimp. Cover and refrigerate for 2–3 hours.
Onion, minced	2 oz.	
Cilantro leaves, chopped fine	3 tbsp.	
Jalapeño, seeded, ribs removed, and minced	1	

Crabmeat, cooked	1 lb.	Just prior to serving, check the crabmeat and remove any cartilage or bits of shell. Add the cleaned crabmeat and mix well.

Serve on a bed of lettuce garnished with slices of avocado and a julienne of roasted and peeled red pepper. May also be served heaped over a halved avocado and garnished with green olives stuffed with pimento.

SHRIMP COCKTAIL   *Dominican Republic*   Yield: 10–12 servings

Sauce:

Onion, peeled, large dice	1½ lb.	Blanche the onions in boiling water for 1 minute. Drain and place in the bowl of a food processor. Using a steel blade, puree the onions until very smooth.

(Continued)

Olive oil	4 oz.
Lime juice, fresh	4 oz.
Tomato, peeled and seeded	8 oz.
Tabasco *or* Pickapeppa sauce*	to taste
Worcestershire sauce	to taste
Salt, black pepper, and sugar	to taste

Add the oil, lime juice, tomato, and seasonings to the onions and continue to process until well blended.

Shrimp, peeled and deveined	4–6 oz. per serving

To prepare an individual serving: Boil or steam shrimp for several minutes, or until they are no longer translucent. Toss the cooked shrimp in a small amount of the sauce.

Serve as an appetizer garnished with lime wedges, or as a light luncheon dish accompanied by a garnish of fresh garden vegetables and slices of hard boiled egg with a small bowl of the sauce alongside.

To prepare in quantity: Cook shrimp as directed and, while still warm, place in the cocktail sauce. Refrigerate until needed.

SALTED COD CAKES— FOUR VERSIONS

Yield: variable, depending on size

Jamaica—"Stamp and Go":

Salt cod, dried	1 lb.

Soak the cod for 24 hours, changing the water several times. When ready to cook, place fish in a saucepan with enough water to cover. Bring to a boil, then lower heat and simmer for 15 minutes. Remove the fish and discard any skin or bones (use only the white portions of the fish). Reserve.

---

*Though these two sauces have very different flavors, each works well. The results, however, are two distinct preparations.

Flour	8 oz.
Baking powder	2 tsp.
Milk	as needed
Eggs, beaten	2
Achiote oil	1 tbsp.
(see the recipe in the "Regional Flavorings" section)	

Mix the flour and baking powder until thoroughly blended. Add enough milk to make a soft dough. Add the eggs and achiote oil and mix well. Reserve.

Scallions, sliced thin, white and green parts	6
Green bell pepper, seeded	12 oz.
Chili pepper, seeded, ribs removed, and minced	to taste
Salt and white pepper	to taste

Place the cod, scallions, peppers, and salt and pepper in the bowl of a food processor, and, using the pulse action, process until texture is smooth but still somewhat grainy. Blend this mixture thoroughly with the reserved dough. Test a spoonful of the mixture by sautéing in hot oil. Adjust seasoning, if necessary.

Form the mixture into cakes and deep-fry at 375 degrees F until golden brown. The size of cakes will vary according to usage: For hors d'oeuvre, shape into small balls; for entrées, shape into flat, oval cakes.

Trinidad — "Accra":

Salt cod, dried	1 lb.

Prepare the salt cod as indicated in the recipe above, shred it, and set aside.

Yeast, active dry	½ oz.
Water, warm	8 oz.

Proof yeast in warm water (110–115 degrees F) for 10–15 minutes.

Flour	8 oz.
Onion, minced	8 oz.
Chives *or* scallions, minced	2 tbsp.
Sugar	2 tbsp.
Garlic, minced	1 tsp.
Salt and white pepper	to taste

Thoroughly mix the reserved fish and the remaining ingredients. Add a generous amount of pepper, but use salt with caution.

Add the yeast mixture, mix well, and set aside in a warm place for an hour or two to allow dough to rise. Using a small ladle, deep-fry at 375 degrees F until golden. Drain on paper toweling before serving.

Puerto Rico — "Bacalaitos Fritos":

Salt cod, dried	1 lb.

Prepare the cod as indicated in the recipe on page 33, shred it, and set aside.

Flour	12 oz.
Baking powder	2 tsp.
Water	2–4 oz. or as needed

Blend the flour and baking powder. Add water to make a soft, moist dough.

Cilantro leaves, fresh, chopped	2 tbsp.
Garlic, minced	2 tsp.
Black pepper, coarsely ground	1 tsp.
Chili pepper, fresh, minced (optional)	1 tsp.

Add the reserved fish and seasonings and mix thoroughly. Shape as needed and deep-fry at 375 degrees F.

Brazil — "Bolinos de Bacalhau":

Salt cod, dried	1 lb.

Prepare the cod as indicated above and set aside.

Potatoes, cooked and mashed	1 lb.
Eggs, beaten	3
Milk	6 oz.

Cook the potatoes in their skins. When done, peel and mash with the eggs and milk. Reserve.

Oil	2 oz.
Onion, minced	4 oz.
Cilantro leaves, fresh, chopped	4 tbsp.
Flour	1 oz.

Heat the oil in a large skillet and sauté the cod. As it cooks, break it into small flakes using a fork. Add the onion, cilantro, and flour, stir well, and cook over low heat for 4–5 minutes.

Nutmeg, grated	½ tsp.
Salt and white pepper	to taste
Milk	as needed

Add the mashed potatoes to the pan along with the seasonings. Blend all ingredients thoroughly. Add additional milk, if needed, to make a smooth, slightly moist mixture that can be shaped into small balls or flat cakes as needed. Deep-fry at 375 degrees F.

CLAM SEVICHE   *Peru*

Yield: 10–12 servings

Shucked clams, Cherrystones or other small- to medium-sized clams	1½ qt.

Open the clams over a strainer placed in a stainless-steel or glass mixing bowl and reserve juice. Rinse the clams. Pour the reserved clam juice through a double layer of cheesecloth into a clean mixing bowl to ensure that no sand or other debris remains. Return the rinsed clams to the clam juice.

Lemon juice	8 oz.
Olive oil	4 oz.
Jalapeños, seeded, ribs removed, and minced	2
Salt and black pepper	to taste

Mix the lemon juice, oil, jalapeños, and salt and pepper and add to the clams. Cover and refrigerate for 2–3 hours.

Potatoes, long white	2½ lb.

Peel, wash, and cut the potatoes into small cubes. Place in boiling water and cook until fork tender. Drain and let cool.

Tomatoes, cubed	2 lb.
Onion, red, thin-sliced	½ lb.

When the potatoes are cool, add them to the clams along with the tomato and onion. Toss well and refrigerate overnight.

Lettuce leaves	as needed
Cilantro leaves, fresh, chopped	as needed

To serve, place a bed of lettuce on a chilled salad plate. Top with a mound of the clam seviche and garnish with chopped cilantro leaves.

CRAB CAKES   *Cuba*   Yield: 10 – 12 servings

Crabmeat, cooked	2½ lb.

Check crabmeat and remove all traces of cartilage or shell. Place cleaned crabmeat in a mixing bowl.

Bread crumbs, dry	3 – 4 oz.
Eggs, beaten	2 large
Cilantro leaves	4 tbsp.
Cumin, ground	2 tsp.
Tabasco sauce	to taste
Salt and white pepper	to taste
Mayonnaise	as needed

Add the bread crumbs, eggs, cilantro, and seasonings and blend thoroughly. Add enough mayonnaise to bind the mixture and make it moist enough to shape into small, firm cakes. Sauté a teaspoon of the mixture in butter and taste. Adjust seasonings, if necessary.

Cornmeal	as needed

Shape the crabmeat mixture into small round or oval flat cakes about a ½ inch thick. Dredge in cornmeal to coat all surfaces of the cakes. Place on sheet pan. If making a large quantity, separate layers with waxed paper. Refrigerate until needed.

Clarified butter	as needed
Papaya chutney (see the recipe in the "Salsa, Condiments, and Dressings" section)	as needed

Sauté the cakes in hot, clarified butter until golden brown on both sides. Serve with a side dish of papaya chutney.

HUEVOS RANCHEROS *Mexico*

Yield: 10–12 servings

Pork/Tomato Sauce:

Vegetable oil *or* lard	2–3 oz.
Pork shoulder, cubed	2 lb.
Onion, diced	1 lb.
Green bell peppers, seeded and chopped	1 lb.
Garlic, minced	3 tbsp.

In a heavy skillet, heat the oil over medium to high heat and brown the pork. When done, place pork in a clean casserole and reserve. Using the same skillet, sauté the onion and green peppers until soft. Add the garlic and sauté for another minute.

Tomatoes, plum, peeled and chopped	2 lb.
Chicken stock	8 oz.
Red wine vinegar	2 oz.
Jalapeños, seeded and minced	3 tsp. or to taste
Oregano, dried	1 tbsp.
Thyme	1 tsp.
Sugar	to taste
Salt and black pepper	to taste

Add the tomatoes to the skillet, and raise the heat to high. When boiling, deglaze the pan. Add the chicken stock, vinegar, jalapeños, herbs, and seasonings and simmer for 20–30 minutes. Adjust seasonings if necessary. Add this to the casserole containing the pork. Mix well. Simmer, partially covered, for 2 hours, or until the pork is tender enough to be shredded. Using two forks, shred the pork and combine with the sauce. Let cool, then refrigerate until needed.

Eggs	as needed
Parsley *or* cilantro leaves, fresh, chopped	as needed

To prepare an individual serving: Place a generous amount of the pork/tomato sauce on the bottom of a large, individual-serving, heat-proof dish. Make two evenly spaced indentations with the back of a spoon and break an egg into each of the indentations. Cover with foil and place in a 400 degree F oven for 5–7 minutes or until the whites are set. Garnish with chopped parsley or cilantro leaves just prior to serving.

(Continued)

A good luncheon or brunch preparation. One egg instead of two may also be served. Accompany with a side dish of cooked pinto, red, or black beans. A few spoons of cooked beans may also be added to the sauce and heated with the eggs. In this case, do not serve the accompanying side dish of beans.

STUFFED POTATOES   *Peru*   Yield: 10–12 servings

Potatoes, all-purpose	5 lb.	
Eggs, beaten	3	
Salt and white pepper	to taste	

Boil potatoes until tender. Let cool, peel, and mash together with the eggs, salt, and white pepper. Reserve.

Vegetable oil	as needed
Onion, minced	12 oz.
Garlic, minced	3 tsp.
Beef,* ground twice	1 lb.

In a heavy skillet, heat the oil over medium heat and sauté the onions until soft. Add the garlic and meat and continue to cook, stirring, until the meat has browned. Place in a colander to drain excess fat, then transfer to a clean mixing bowl.

Eggs, hard boiled and chopped	4
Olives, black, pitted and chopped	20
Raisins	4 tbsp.
Cumin	1 tsp.
Salt and black pepper	to taste

Add the eggs, olives, raisins, and seasonings to the meat mixture and mix thoroughly. Reserve.

Divide the mashed potatoes into equal, disclike portions resembling pancakes, large enough to cover the palm of your hand. Place a small spoonful of the meat mixture in the center, leaving enough potato surrounding the meat to allow it to be folded over and sealed. Moisten hands and shape the stuffed potato so that it resembles an egg. When all of the potato "pancakes" have been stuffed and shaped, place them on a lightly oiled sheet pan, cover, and refrigerate until needed.

---

*Other meats may be substituted.

Flour	as needed
Egg, beaten	as needed
Bread crumbs	as needed
Lemon wedges	as needed

To serve, dredge stuffed potatoes in flour, egg, then bread crumbs, and deep-fry at 375 degrees F until golden brown. Drain on paper or clean kitchen towels and serve garnished with lemon wedges.

Make in larger sizes for a luncheon or light dinner entrée. Serve with a mixed green salad containing sliced tomatoes, black olives, and diced onions.

EGGS WITH TOMATO AND SALT COD   *Brazil*

Yield: 10 servings

Salt cod, dried	1½ lb.
Milk	as needed
Water	as needed

Soak the salt cod for 24 hours, changing the water several times. Place the fish in a saucepan and cover with a 50/50 mixture of milk and water. Bring to a boil, then lower the heat and simmer for 15 minutes or until the fish flakes easily. Remove the fish and discard any skin or bones. Reserve fish and discard the cooking liquid.

Béchamel:

Butter	2 oz.
Flour	3 oz.
Milk, scalded	1 qt.

In a small saucepan melt the butter, then add and blend in the flour. Cook over low heat, stirring, for 3–4 minutes. Slowly add the scalded milk and simmer, stirring, until thickened. Reserve.

Olive oil	2 oz.
Onion, minced	1 lb.
Tomatoes, peeled, seeded, and chopped	1 lb.

In a saucepan large enough to hold the combined ingredients, heat the oil over medium heat and sauté the onion until very soft. Add the tomatoes and cook until thickened.

Capers	2 tbsp.
Salt and white pepper	to taste

Add the béchamel, cod, and capers and mix gently until well blended. Let cool and reserve.

(Continued)

Butter	as needed
Eggs	2 per serving
Parmesan cheese, grated	as needed

To serve: Place a layer of the cod/tomato mixture in an oven-proof, individual-serving dish that has been lightly buttered. Make two indentations with the back of a spoon and place an egg in each. Top with a sprinkling of grated cheese. Bake in a 400 degree F oven until the yolks are set but not firm.

Serve as a luncheon entrée accompanied by a garden salad. A single-egg portion can be served as an appetizer.

QUESO FLAMEADO   *Mexico*

Yield: 1 serving

Chorizo, chopped	2 oz.
Queso asadero *or* fresh mozzarella, grated	2–3 oz.
Brandy, warmed	1 oz.

Sauté the chorizo until browned. Place the cheese in an individual-portion, ovenproof serving dish. Sprinkle the chorizo on top and place under the broiler 6–8 inches from the flame. When cheese has melted, but not browned, remove from broiler.

Pour warmed brandy on top and ignite. This may be done tableside. Serve with tortillas and salsa. This may be prepared easily for two or more persons.

OYSTERS SEVICHE   *Guatemala*

Yield: 10 servings

Oysters, shucked, liquids strained	5 dozen
Tomato, peeled, seeded, and chopped	1½ lb.
Onion, small dice	8 oz.
Lemon juice	8 oz.
Mint leaves, fresh, chopped	4 tbsp.
Hot pepper flakes	1 tsp.
Salt and white pepper	to taste

Combine all ingredients along with the oyster liquids, and let marinate overnight under refrigeration.

Remove the oyster mixture from the marinade using a slotted spoon, and serve, six oysters per serving, on a chilled plate. Garnish with cucumbers, black and green olives, green bell pepper rings, or other garden vegetables in season. Use some of the marinade as a dressing for the vegetable garnish.

SHRIMP IN RUM SAUCE *Barbados*

Yield: 1 serving

Shrimp	2 – 3 oz. per serving
Flour	as needed
Butter, clarified	as needed

Peel the shrimp leaving the tail section intact; then devein and butterfly. Dredge in flour, shake off any excess, and panfry in clarified butter until just pink. Remove to a warm platter.

Butter, whole	1 tsp.
Mayonnaise	1 tbsp.
Honey	1 tsp.
Rum, dark	2 tsp.

Discard any clarified butter left in the pan. Add the whole butter and heat until melted. Then add the mayonnaise, honey, and rum and, stirring, heat through.

Lettuce, shredded	as needed
Cilantro, fresh, *or* watercress	as needed

Place shrimp on a bed of shredded lettuce and pour sauce on top. Garnish with sprigs of cilantro or watercress.

(Continued)

SHRIMP WITH CHILI SAUCE   *Mexico*

Yield: 10 servings

Chili Sauce:

Olive oil	6 oz.
Lime juice, fresh squeezed	8 oz.
Poblanos or serranos,* seeded, ribs removed, and minced fine	3 – 4 or to taste
Cilantro leaves, fresh, chopped	12 sprigs
Garlic, minced	1 tsp.
Oregano, dried	1 tbsp.
Salt and white pepper	to taste

Combine the oil, lime juice, chilies, herbs, and seasonings, and reserve.

Water	2 qt.
Onion, quartered	1 large
Celery	4 ribs
Bay leaf	2
Salt	2 tbsp.
Peppercorns, black	1 tbsp.

In a stockpot large enough to hold the shrimp, combine the water, onion, celery, bay leaf, and seasonings and bring to a boil. Lower heat and simmer for 30 minutes. (Do not add shrimp at this time.)

Shrimp, cleaned, deveined, butterflied	4 lb. (number used per serving will depend on size)

Add shrimp. Cook briefly, until they begin to turn pink. (Do not overcook the shrimp.) When done, place shrimp immediately in ice water to cool. When cool, drain and combine with the chili sauce. Mix well to ensure that the shrimp are well coated. Refrigerate until needed.

Serve on a bed of chopped romaine or other assertive greens. Garnish with cubes of fresh mozzarella and black olives.

---

*Other hot, green chilies may be substituted, to taste.

CODFISH WITH ACKEE   *Jamaica*

Yield: 10–12 servings

Salt cod	2½ lb.

Soak the cod for 24 hours, changing the water several times. When ready to cook, place the fish in a saucepan with enough water to cover. Bring to a boil, then lower heat and simmer for 15 minutes. Remove fish and discard any skin or bones. Drain well, and when cool enough to handle, break the fish into flakes. Reserve.

Salt pork *or* slab bacon, small dice	6 oz.
Onions, diced	1¼ lb.
Hot peppers, fresh, seeded and sliced thin	to taste

In a large skillet, sauté the salt pork or bacon until all of the fat has been rendered. Remove bits from pan and reserve. Add the onions and hot peppers and sauté until soft.

Tomatoes, peeled and chopped	1½ lb.
Ackee (available canned)	2–2½ lb.
Black pepper, coarsely ground	to taste
Salt	if needed

Add the reserved cod, tomatoes, ackee, and black pepper. Cover pan and simmer for 10 minutes. Add salt at this point if necessary.

Green bell pepper, thinly sliced	as needed

When serving, garnish the cod with pork or bacon bits and a sprinkling of thinly sliced green bell pepper.

AVOCADO STUFFED WITH SHRIMP SEVICHE   *Mexico*

Yield: 10 servings

Shrimp, medium, peeled, deveined and butterflied, tails left on	2½ lb.
Tomato, peeled, seeded and chopped	1½ lb.
Onion, red, chopped fine	½ lb.
Red bell pepper, roasted, peeled, sliced julienne	½ lb.
Jalapeño peppers, seeded and chopped fine	2
Lime or lemon juice, fresh squeezed	1 pint
Olive oil	4 oz.
Green olives, pitted and coarsely chopped	20
Cilantro leaves, chopped	20 sprigs or to taste
Salt and pepper, black	to taste

Combine these ingredients in a glass or stainless steel container and marinate, overnight, in the refrigerator. If the shrimp still appear to look raw, marinate longer.

Lettuce, romaine, shredded	as needed
Avocados, marinated	5 large as needed
Lemon juice	as needed

To serve cover a chilled plate with a bed of shredded lettuce or with the whole leaves, if desired. Cut an avocado in half, remove pit and rub the cut surfaces with fresh lemon juice. Using a slotted spoon fill the cavity of the avocado with the marinated shrimp mixture allowing the mixture to spill over the sides of the avocado.

Garnish with sliced tomato, cucumber, and radishes or any other seasonal, fresh vegetables. A complete luncheon entrée.

JICAMA WITH CHILI AND LIME   *Mexico*

Yield: 10 servings

Jicama	2 small
Chili powder	as needed, mild or hot
Salt	as needed

Cut the jicama in quarters. Using a paring knife, remove the outer skin and the under layer, which is the same color as the skin. Cut the quarters into smaller, bite sized pieces. Place the jicama in an attractive pattern on a small plate. Sprinkle lightly with chili powder and salt.

Lime wedges	as needed

Garnish with wedges of fresh lime to be used according to taste.

A traditional accompaniment with drinks. Jicama can also be used as a base for hors d'oeuvres. It can be cut into a variety of shapes or shredded, eaten raw or cooked. It retains its crunchiness well and will not, under normal serving conditions, discolor.

SOUPS

SHRIMP AND CLAM SOUP   *Brazil*

Yield: 10 – 12 servings

Clams, small, in shell	40 – 45
Fish stock	16 oz.

Place well-scrubbed clams in fish stock and bring to a rapid boil. When clams have opened, remove them and reserve. Decant the pot liquids by straining through several layers of cheesecloth. Add to the resulting pot liquids enough fish stock to make 1½ qt. Reserve clams and stock separately.

Olive oil	2 oz.
Onion, chopped	1½ lb.
Jalapeños, seeded and chopped fine	2
Garlic, minced	1 tbsp.
Turmeric	2 tsp.

Heat oil in a small soup pot over low to medium heat. Sauté the onion until soft. Add the jalapeños and garlic and continue to cook for another minute. Do not allow vegetables to brown. Add the turmeric, stir well, and cook for another minute.

Coconut milk, thin	1 qt.
Salt and white pepper	to taste

Add reserved fish stock and coconut milk to soup pot and simmer for 10 – 15 minutes. Add salt and pepper to taste. Let cool and reserve.

Shrimp, peeled and deveined	2 – 3 per serving, depending on size
Lemon juice	as needed
Cayenne pepper	as needed

To serve: Reheat soup as needed. Just before serving, add 2 – 3 shrimp and 3 – 4 clams in the shell per serving. Heat until the shrimp have just turned pink and the clams are heated through.

Add a squeeze of fresh lemon juice and a scant sprinkling of cayenne pepper to each heated bowl before serving.

RED BELL PEPPER SOUP   *Mexico*

Yield: 10 – 12 servings

Red bell peppers, halved and seeded	3 lb.

Place the peppers cut side down on a lightly oiled sheet pan. Place in a 400 degree F oven and roast until the skins begin to char. Remove from heat, cover with a towel, and let rest for 5 minutes. Remove skins from the peppers and reserve.

(Continued)

Oil, olive *or* corn	2 oz.	Heat oil over medium heat and sauté the onions until very soft but not browned. Place the onions and the roasted peppers in the bowl of a food processor and, using a steel blade, puree until very smooth.
Onion, sliced	1½ lb.	

Chicken stock	2 qt.	In a small soup pot, bring the stock and the tomato to a boil. Add the onion/red pepper puree and the jalapeño peppers. Lower heat and simmer for 15 minutes. Remove the jalapeños and discard. Add salt and pepper to taste.
Tomato, peeled, seeded, and chopped	8 oz.	
Jalapeños, washed and left whole	1–2	
Salt and black pepper	to taste	

Serve hot, garnished with a dollop of sour cream.

SHRIMP SOUP *Panama*   Yield: 10 servings

Vegetable oil	2 tbsp.	In a soup pot, heat the oil over low to medium heat and sauté the onion and bell pepper until they are soft. Add the tomato paste and mix well. Cook for another minute, then add the tomatoes and simmer for 5 minutes.
Onion, diced	1 lb.	
Bell pepper, green, small dice	12 oz.	
Tomato paste	1 tbsp.	
Tomatoes, peeled and chopped	2 lb.	

Fish stock	2 qt.	Add the fish stock and bring to a boil. Skim if necessary, then add salt and pepper to taste. Lower heat and simmer for 20 minutes, partially covered.
Salt and black pepper	to taste	

Yams	1½ lb.	Peel yams and cut into small dice. Cook in boiling water until tender. Mash half of the cubes and add to reserved fish soup. Mix well and simmer for another 5 minutes. When done, let cool and reserve. Reserve the remaining yam cubes for garnish.

Vermicelli	1 oz. per serving
Shrimp, medium, peeled and deveind	4 per serving

To serve, bring the reserved fish soup to a boil as needed. Add a serving of vermicelli and cook until just tender. Add the shrimp and cook briefly, until just pink. Garnish with the reserved yam cubes.

SHRIMP DUMPLINGS IN TOMATO AND FISH BROTH *Mexico*

Yield: 10–12 servings

Shrimp Dumplings:

Vegetable oil	2 tbsp.
Onion, minced	8 oz.
Tomato, peeled, seeded, and chopped fine	8 oz.
Oregano, dried	1 tsp. or to taste
Salt and white pepper	to taste

In a heavy skillet, heat the oil over moderate heat and sauté the onion until soft. Add the tomato, oregano, salt, and pepper and cook for 5 minutes over low heat. When done, transfer contents to the bowl of a food processor.

Shrimp, raw, peeled, deveined, and chopped	1½ lb.
Egg yolks	3
Flour	as needed

Add the shrimp and puree until smooth. Add the egg yolks and mix thoroughly using the pulse action. Transfer to a clean mixing bowl and add enough flour to form a slightly moist, doughlike mixture. Reserve, covered, in the refrigerator until needed.

Fish Broth:

Vegetable oil	as needed
Onion, sliced in thin rings	1 lb.
Tomato, peeled and chopped	2 lb.
Chilies, green, seeded, ribs removed, and sliced in thin strips	3 or to taste
Fish stock	2½ qt.
Salt and black pepper	to taste

In a small soup pot, heat the oil over medium heat and sauté the onion until soft. Add the tomatoes and chilies and cook over low heat 3–4 minutes more. Add the fish stock and seasonings and simmer for 30 minutes. When done, strain the stock, discard the solids, and reserve.

(Continued)

Coriander leaves, fresh, chopped	as needed
Limes, quartered	as needed

To prepare an individual serving: Bring 7–8 ounces of the fish broth to a boil. Lower heat to a simmer and poach 2–3 rounded spoonfuls of the dumpling mixture for 5–6 minutes, depending on size. Pour into a heated bowl and garnish with fresh, chopped coriander. Serve lime wedges on the side.

CREAMED PUMPKIN SOUP   *Jamaica*

Yield: 10–12 servings

Butter	8 oz.
Onions, small dice	1 lb.

In a small soup pot, heat butter, add onions, and cook over low heat until the onions are very soft but not brown.

Pumpkin *or* squash,* cut into cubes	3 lb.
Chicken stock	2 qt.
Salt and white pepper	to taste

Add the pumpkin or squash and chicken stock. Bring to a boil and skim. Lower heat and simmer, partially covered, until the pumpkin is very soft. Remove the pumpkin and puree in a food processor. Return the pulp to the stock. Adjust for salt and pepper and reserve.

Heavy cream	as needed
Tabasco *or* any other hot sauce	as needed
Nutmeg, freshly grated	as needed

To prepare an individual serving: Reheat pumpkin soup. Add 1 part heavy cream to 3 parts pumpkin soup. Garnish with a dash of hot sauce and a sprinkling of nutmeg.

*Winter squash such as acorn, butternut, or hubbard may be used.

POTATO AND POBLANO SOUP   *Mexico*

Yield: 10–12 servings

Vegetable oil	2 tbsp.
Onion, chopped	1 lb.
Garlic, minced	2 tsp.
Poblano chilies, roasted, peeled, seeds removed, and chopped	6
Tomato, peeled, seeded, and chopped	1½ lb.

In a small soup pot, heat the oil over medium heat and sauté the onions until soft. Add the garlic and chilies and continue to cook for another 2–3 minutes. Add the tomatoes, mix well, simmer for 5 minutes more.

Chicken stock	2½ qt.
Potatoes, boiling, peeled and cubed	1½ lb.
Oregano *or* other fresh herb, fresh, chopped	to taste
Sharp cheddar, grated	as needed

Add the chicken stock and potatoes and simmer until the potatoes are tender. Garnish each serving with a sprinkling of oregano leaves and grated sharp cheddar.

SPICY PEANUT SOUP
St. Croix

Yield: 10–12 servings

Vegetable oil	3 oz.
Onion, small dice	1½ lb.
Peanut butter, unsweetened	1 lb.

In a small soup pot, heat the oil over low heat and sauté the onion until very soft and beginning to color. Add peanut butter and cook, stirring, for 6–8 minutes or until the peanut butter becomes very soft and mixes thoroughly with the onion.

(Continued)

Chicken stock	2 qt.
Milk, evaporated	12 oz.
Light cream	8 oz.
White pepper	1–2 tbsp.
Cayenne pepper	1½ tsp. or to taste
Sherry, dry	8 oz.
Salt	to taste

Add the chicken stock and combine thoroughly. Add the remaining ingredients and simmer, partially covered, for 30–40 minutes.

Garnish each serving with a dollop of whipped cream and a sprinkling of crushed peanuts.

PEANUT SOUP   *St. Kitts*

Yield: 10–12 servings

Chicken, stewing, *or* legs and thighs from fowl	5 lb.
Water	2 qt.

In a soup pot, simmer chicken until very tender, skimming liquid as needed. When done, let chicken cool in the broth. When cool enough to handle, remove chicken from bones. Discard all skin and fat. Reserve meat and degrease broth and reserve.

Peanut butter	10 oz.
Scallions, white and tender green parts	6 oz.
Bell's Poultry Seasoning	2 tbsp.
Ginger root, fresh, grated	2 tbsp.
Nutmeg, ground	1 tsp.
Allspice, ground	1 tsp.

Place all of the remaining ingredients into the bowl of a food processor and puree. Add the cooked chicken and enough of the broth to the contents in the bowl of the processor to puree to a smooth consistency. In a soup pot, combine this puree with the remaining broth and simmer for 20–30 minutes.

Coconut milk, thin	1 pint or more
Chili sauce	to taste
Salt and black pepper	to taste

Add the coconut milk, chili sauce, and salt and pepper. Adjust consistency, if desired, with more coconut milk. Heat through. Do not boil. Serve hot.

Prior to serving, add a small amount of dark rum to each bowl and top with toasted croutons.

KIDNEY BEAN SOUP   *Cuba*   Yield: 10–12 servings

Kidney beans	1½ lb.

Wash the beans, remove any debris, and soak in water overnight. Rinse well and discard the water.

Vegetable oil *or* lard	2 oz.
Onion, chopped	1 lb.
Carrots, sliced	12 oz.
Garlic, minced	1 tbsp.

In a soup pot, heat the oil over medium heat and cook the vegetables, covered, until soft.

Chicken stock *or* water	2½ qt.
Tomatoes, peeled and chopped	2 lb.
Ham hocks, skin removed	2
Parsley	5–6 sprigs

Add the stock or water to the pot and bring to a boil. Add the beans, tomatoes, ham hocks, and parsley and simmer for 1½ to 2 hours, or until the beans are tender.

Salt and black pepper	to taste
Cilantro leaves, fresh, chopped	as needed

When done, remove the ham hocks and cut the meat from the bone. Reserve. Remove the parsley sprigs and discard. Strain the soup, reserving the liquid in a clean soup pot. Degrease the liquid. Place the cooked beans in the bowl of a food processor and puree. Combine the pureed beans and the reserved meat from the ham hocks with the broth. Mix well and add salt and pepper to taste. Serve, hot, garnished with chopped, fresh cilantro leaves.

CORN CHOWDER WITH ROASTED CHILIES   *Mexico*

Yield: 10–12 servings

Poblano chilies	5–6 or to taste

Brush the chilies lightly with oil and place them close to the broiler flame, turning frequently, until the skins begin to blister. Cover and let steam for a few minutes. When cool enough to handle, split in half, discard the stem and seeds, and peel. Dice chilies and reserve.

Butter, sweet	4 oz.
Onion, minced	12 oz.
Garlic, minced	3 tsp.

Heat the butter until it foams. Reduce heat to low and sauté the onion until soft but not brown. Add the garlic and cook for another minute. When done, place the onion and garlic in the bowl of a food processor.

Corn, fresh, stripped from the cob	9–10 ears (approximately 2 lb. cut corn)
Cornstarch	4 tsp.
Water	as needed

Add the fresh corn to the food processor bowl and puree until smooth. Add the cornstarch dissolved in a small amount of water and mix thoroughly.

Butter, sweet	2 oz.
Milk	1½ qt.
Salt and white pepper	to taste
Sugar	to taste

Melt the butter in a small soup pot and add the corn mixture. Cook, stirring, over medium heat until the puree thickens. Add the milk and mix well. Simmer for 15–20 minutes. Add the salt, pepper, and sugar. Let cool and reserve. The soup may be strained at this point if a very smooth texture is desired.

Heavy cream	as needed
Queso fresco *or* farmer's cheese	as needed
Parsley leaves, fresh, chopped	as needed

To prepare one or more servings: Heat two parts of the corn chowder to one part heavy cream. When done, garnish with diced chili, a few bits of cheese, and chopped parsley.

CHICKEN AVOCADO SOUP   *Mexico*

Yield: 10–12 servings

Stewing fowl	5–6 lb.
Water *or* chicken stock	3 qt.
Onion, quartered	1 lb.
Carrot, thick sliced	½ lb.
Celery, cut in half	3 stalks
Chilies, hot, red, dried	4
Garlic, chopped	3 cloves
Oregano	1 tbsp.
Cumin seed, crushed	1 tsp.
Salt	to taste

Truss the fowl and place in a soup pot with the water or stock. Bring to a boil, then lower heat and simmer for about 30 minutes. Skim as necessary. When the liquid is clear add the vegetables, herbs, and seasonings and continue to simmer for another 1½ hours, or until the fowl is very tender. Let cool in broth. Remove the fowl and strip the meat from the bones. Discard the skin and bones. Strain the broth and discard the solids. Cut the chicken into bite-sized pieces, cover with plastic wrap and refrigerate. Refrigerate the broth. When the broth has congealed, remove and discard the solidified fat. If too much of the broth has evaporated during cooking, add more stock to bring the level up to 2½ qt.

Green beans, trimmed and cut in 1-inch lengths	1 lb.
Tomatoes, peeled, seeded, and chopped	2 lb.
Salt and black pepper	to taste

Heat the broth to a boil. Add the green beans and tomatoes and cook for 5 minutes, or until the beans are just tender. Return the cooked chicken to the pot and heat through. Adjust seasoning with salt and pepper.

When serving, garnish with fresh, chopped cilantro leaves and thin slices of avocado. Serve wedges of fresh lime on the side.

CHICKEN SOUP WITH LIME   *Mexico*

Yield: 10–12 servings

Chicken stock	3 qt.
Onions, cut in quarters	1 lb.
Garlic, chopped	5 cloves
Black peppercorns	1 tsp.
Thyme	to taste
Salt	to taste

Place the stock, onions, garlic, and seasonings in a soup pot and bring to a boil. Lower heat and simmer, partially covered, for 30 minutes.

(Continued)

Chicken breasts, skin off, bone in	1 lb.
Chicken livers, trimmed	1 lb.

Add the chicken breasts and poach them over low heat for 10–12 minutes, depending on the thickness of the meat. Add the chicken livers 3–4 minutes before the breast meat is done. Remove from heat and let cool in the broth. When cool enough to handle, shred the chicken and chop the livers fine. Reserve. Pour the broth through a double layer of cheesecloth and reserve in a separate container.

Vegetable oil	1 oz.
Serrano chilies, seeded and chopped	2 or to taste
Onion, small dice	1 lb.
Tomatoes, peeled and chopped	1½ lb.

Heat the oil in the same soup pot and sauté the chilies and onion until soft. Add the tomatoes and cook for another 5 minutes. Return the chicken broth to the pot.

Lime juice	6 oz. or to taste
Salt and black pepper	to taste
Cilantro leaves, chopped	as needed

Add the reserved chicken and livers and lime juice and simmer for 15 minutes. Add salt and pepper. When serving, add a tablespoon of chopped, fresh cilantro leaves to each bowl.

Garnish with wedges of toasted or deep-fried tortilla strips, avocado slices, and lime.

BLACK BEAN SOUP— VERSION 1   *Cuba*

Yield: 10–12 servings

Black beans	1 lb.

Wash beans and remove any debris. Soak beans in water overnight. Rinse well and discard the water.

Chicken stock	2½ qt.

Place the beans in a soup pot with the chicken stock. Bring to a boil, then lower heat and simmer for 1½ to 2 hours, or until the beans are tender. Remove approximately one-third of the beans and puree in a food processor. Return the pureed beans to the pot.

Lard *or* vegetable oil	2 tbsp.
Onion, small dice	1 lb.
Green bell pepper, small dice	8 oz.
Hot pepper, green, fresh, minced	2 tbsp.
Coriander leaves, fresh, chopped	10 sprigs
Oregano, dried	2 tbsp.
Cumin, ground	2 tsp.

In a separate skillet heat the fat and lightly sauté the onion and peppers until soft. Add the herbs and cumin powder to the pan and cook for 1–2 minutes. When done add to the soup pot.

Cloves	10–15
Orange, washed and unpeeled	1 large
Salt and black pepper	to taste
Stock	if needed

Insert cloves into the skin of the orange and add to the soup pot. Add salt and pepper and simmer for 25–30 minutes. When done, remove the orange and adjust seasonings if necessary. Add more stock if the consistency is too thick.

Serve with a garnish of chopped onion and chopped hard boiled egg.

BLACK BEAN SOUP— VERSION 2   *Puerto Rico*

Yield: 10–12 servings

Black beans	1 lb.
Ham hocks	4

Wash beans and remove any debris. Soak beans overnight, then rinse well and place in a soup pot with 2 qt. of water along with the ham hocks. Simmer for 2 hours, or until the beans are very tender. Remove the ham hocks; when cool enough to handle, separate the meat from the bone, skin, and fat. Degrease the liquid in the pot. Cut the meat into small pieces and return it to the soup pot.

(Continued)

Vegetable oil	2 tbsp.
Onion, small dice	1 lb.
Garlic, minced	1 tbsp.
Tomato paste	3 oz.
Allspice, ground	1 tsp.
Mace, ground	1 tsp.
Chili sauce	to taste

Heat the oil in a skillet and sauté the onions over low heat until soft. Add the remaining ingredients and continue to cook for several minutes more. Add this mixture to the soup pot and simmer for 30–40 minutes.

Garnish with chopped, fresh cilantro.

BLACK BEAN SOUP— VERSION 3   *Brazil*

Yield: 10–12 servings

Black beans	12 oz.

Wash the beans, remove any debris, and soak in water overnight. Discard the water and rinse beans well.

Butter, whole	2 oz.
Onion, chopped fine	1 lb.
Tomato paste	3 tbsp.
Beef stock	2½ qt.

In a soup pot, heat the butter over medium heat and sauté the onion until soft. Add the tomato paste, mix well, and cook over low heat for 2–3 minutes. Add the stock and stir well.

Salt	1 tbsp. or to taste
Black pepper	1 tsp. or to taste

Add the beans and salt and pepper. Cook over low to medium heat, partially covered, until the beans are tender.

Pumpkin, cooked	1 lb.
Salt and black pepper	as needed
Lemon, quartered	as needed

Place half of the beans in the bowl of a food processor. Add the cooked pumpkin, and, using a steel blade, puree until smooth. Return this puree to the soup pot and mix well. Simmer for 10–15 minutes. Adjust for salt and pepper. Serve with lemon wedges.

AVOCADO SOUP—THREE VERSIONS

Yield: 10–12 servings

Version 1—Caribbean:

Avocado pulp	1½ lb.
Heavy cream	1 pt.

Scoop the pulp from the avocados and, using a steel blade, puree to a smooth consistency in a food processor. Add the heavy cream and blend thoroughly.

Chicken stock	1½ qt.
Tabasco sauce	to taste
Salt and black pepper	to taste

Pour the chicken stock through a double layer of cheesecloth, then mix with the avocado and heavy cream. Add the tabasco and salt and pepper. Serve chilled.

Version 2—Nevis:

Avocado pulp	1 lb.
Scallions, white and tender green parts, chopped	6

Puree the avocado pulp and the scallions in a food processor.

Chicken stock	1½ qt.
Heavy cream	12 oz.
Sour cream	12 oz.
Lime juice	4 oz.
Salt	to taste
Black pepper	2 tsp.
Parsley, fresh, chopped	as needed
Lime, quartered	as needed

Add the stock, heavy cream, sour cream, lime juice, salt, and pepper and blend thoroughly. Chill well before serving. Garnish with chopped, fresh parsley and serve with lime wedges on the side.

(Continued)

Version 3 — Peru:

Olive oil	2 oz.
Onion, small dice	1 lb.
Celery, small dice	4 oz.
Jalapeños, seeded, ribs removed, and minced	2 whole
Coriander, ground	1 tsp. or to taste

In a heavy-bottomed soup pot, heat the oil over medium heat. Add the vegetables and coriander and sauté until the vegetables are very soft, but do not allow them to brown.

Garlic, minced	2 tsp.
Chicken stock	2 qt.
Cilantro, fresh	6–8 sprigs

Add the garlic and continue to cook for another minute. Then add the stock and cilantro. Raise heat to high and bring to a boil. Lower heat and simmer for 10 minutes, skimming as needed.

Avocado pulp	1 lb.
Salt and white pepper	to taste
Lemon juice	to taste

When soup is done, strain the liquid and place the solids into the bowl of a food processor. Using a steel blade, puree the vegetables, adding the pulp of the avocado a small amount at a time. Add small amounts of the reserved liquid from time to time if the puree becomes too thick. When puree is very smooth combine with the remaining liquid and adjust salt and pepper. Add a small amount of lemon juice if desired. Mix well and chill.

To serve, garnish with a dollop of heavy cream and chopped, fresh cilantro leaves or small cubes of avocado that have been tossed in fresh lemon juice.

PUMPKIN SOUP WITH SHRIMP *Mexico*

Yield: 10–12 servings

Milk	1½ qt.

In a small heavy soup pot, scald the milk over low to medium heat (about 180 degrees F).

Pumpkin, fresh	3 lb.
Chicken stock	1 qt.
Celery, diced	8 oz.
Salt and white pepper	to taste

Peel the pumpkin, discard seeds, and cut flesh into small cubes. Add the pumpkin, chicken stock, celery, and salt and pepper to the milk. Bring to a boil, then lower heat and simmer for 20–30 minutes, or until the pumpkin is very soft. Strain the soup. Return the liquid to the soup pot; then, using a food processor or a food mill, puree the vegetables. Return the puree to the pot and reserve.

Shrimp, peeled and deveined	1 lb.
Lime juice	1 oz.
Nutmeg, grated	to taste
Salt and white pepper	to taste

Using a food processor fitted with a steel blade, puree the shrimp with the lime juice and add to the soup. Simmer for 10 minutes, then add nutmeg to taste. Adjust for salt and pepper.

Garnish with thin slices of lime and chopped, fresh parsley.

PUMPKIN SOUP   *Haiti*

Yield: 10–12 servings

Butter, whole, sweet	4 oz.
Onion, sliced	1½ lb.
Bread crumbs, white, fresh	8 oz.
Chicken stock	2½ qt.

Melt butter in a small soup pot over low to medium heat. Add the onions and cook, stirring occasionally, until the onions begin to color slightly. Add the bread crumbs and cook for another minute. Add the stock and let simmer.

Parsley, flat leaf	5–6 sprigs
Garlic	2 cloves
Jalapeño, seeded, ribs removed, and minced	½

On a chopping board, chop the parsley leaves fine. Mash the garlic with the side of a knife and place on top of the parsley. Add the jalapeño and salt and chop these ingredients as fine as possible to a pureed consistency. Add this mixture to the soup.

(Continued)

Pumpkin, peeled and cubed	1½
Salt and white pepper	to taste

Add the pumpkin and cook until tender. Strain and reserve the stock. Place the pumpkin in the bowl of a food processor fitted with a steel blade and puree. Return the pureed pumpkin to the stock, mix well, and adjust salt and pepper.

Serve with a dollop of heavy cream on top and a sprinkling of chopped, fresh parsley.

PEANUT SOUP   *Ecuador*   Yield: 10–12 servings

Peanuts, roasted, unsalted and shelled	¾ lb.

Place the peanuts in the bowl of a food processor and, using the steel blade, chop the nuts as fine as possible. Reserve in the bowl of the processor.

Potatoes	1 lb.
Chicken stock	2 qt.

Peel and cut the potatoes into cubes. Place in a small soup pot along with the chicken stock and bring to a boil. Lower heat and simmer until the potatoes are tender. Using a skimmer or strainer, remove the cooked potatoes and add to the chopped peanuts. Keep the stock on low heat.

Butter, whole	3 oz.
Onion, diced	1 lb.
Salt and white pepper	to taste

In a separate skillet heat the butter over medium heat and sauté the onion until just soft. Add the onion and the butter to the ingredients in the processor. Puree until very smooth. Add this puree to the stock and simmer for another 10 minutes. Add salt and pepper. Let cool and reserve.

Heavy cream	1 pt.
Salt and white pepper	to taste

Prior to serving, add heavy cream and salt and pepper to taste. If preparing individual servings, add approximately 1 to 1½ ounces of cream per serving. Heat soup through to serving temperature, but do not boil.

Garnish with finely chopped scallions or chives.

KALE SOUP WITH CHORIZO *Brazil*

Yield: 10–12 servings

Kale	2 lb.

Wash the kale, then cut off the stem ends and set aside. Using a vegetable peeler, strip away the back of the stems attached to the leafy parts. Reserve the peelings. Cut the remaining leafy portions across the stems into 1-inch strips. Reserve.

Olive oil	2 oz.
Leeks, white parts, chopped	1 lb.
Garlic, minced	2 tbsp.

In a small soup pot, heat the oil and sauté the leeks over low heat until soft. Do not allow to brown. Add the garlic and cook for another minute. Add the reserved, chopped kale stems and stem peelings and cook for another minute.

Chicken stock	2½ qt.
Idaho potatoes, thin sliced	1 lb.
Bay leaf	2
Cilantro, fresh	6 sprigs
Nutmeg, ground	to taste
Salt and black pepper	to taste

Add the chicken stock, potatoes, and seasonings and simmer, skimming as necessary, for 25–30 minutes. When done, strain the liquid. Using a food processor, puree the vegetables. Return the pureed vegetables to the stock. Reserve.

Olive oil	as needed
Chorizo,* small dice	¾ lb.

As close to serving time as possible, heat a small amount of oil in a large sauté pan and sauté the chorizo over high heat until cooked through. Add the kale leaves and continue to sauté, stirring until the leaves have wilted. Do not overcook. Add this mixture to the soup and combine well. Serve in large, warm soup bowls garnished with a few fresh cilantro leaves.

*If chorizo is unavailable, substitute any spicy garlic sausage.

FISH SOUP WITH SALSA CRUDA   *Mexico*

Yield: 10–12 servings

Vegetable oil	2 oz.
Onion, small dice	1 lb.
Garlic, minced	1 tbsp.
Carrot, small dice	8 oz.
Celery, small dice	8 oz.

In a small soup pot, heat the oil over medium heat and sauté the onions until they begin to get soft. Add the garlic, carrots, and celery and cook for several more minutes.

Fish stock	2 qt.
Tomatoes, peeled and chopped	2½ lb.
Bay leaf	2
Salt and black pepper	to taste

Add the stock, tomatoes, and seasonings and bring to a boil. Lower heat and simmer uncovered for 30 minutes. Let cool and reserve. Remove the bay leaf.

Fish, white, firm-fleshed (cod, monk, or flounder)	1½ lb.
Shrimp, medium, peeled, deveined, and butterflied	1½ lb.
Oysters, shucked, liquor reserved and decanted	24

Trim fish and fillet. Cut into 1-inch cubes. Prepare the shrimp and the oysters, then add the decanted oyster liquor to the soup. Refrigerate the fish and shellfish until needed.

Potato, boiling, cut in small cubes	1½ lb.

Place the potatoes in boiling water and cook until barely tender. Let cool and reserve.

Salsa Cruda (see the recipes in the "Salsas, Condiments, and Dressings" section)	as needed
Avocado, cubed, tossed in fresh lemon juice	as needed

To prepare an individual serving: Bring 6–8 oz. of soup to a boil in a small saucepan. Add a heaping tablespoon of the potato cubes and cook for a minute. Then add 2 oz. of fish, 3 shrimp, and 2 oysters, and continue to cook for another minute. Do not overcook. Pour soup into large, heated soup bowls. Place a spoonful of room-temperature Salsa Cruda on top along with 5–6 small cubes of fresh avocado.

A complete luncheon entrée. Serve with crusty bread and a green salad. If served as a first course, reduce portions.

CHICKEN SOUP LAS TABLAS *Panama*

Yield: 12 servings

Chickens	two 2½-lb. birds

Cut each chicken into six pieces. Trim any excess skin or fat. Place in a single layer in a glass or stainless-steel pan.

Garlic, minced	2 tbsp.
Cilantro, leaves fresh, chopped	6 tbsp.
Oregano	1 tbsp.
Salt	1 tsp.
Black pepper	1 tsp.
Corn oil *or* olive oil	as needed

Combine the garlic, herbs, and seasonings with enough oil to bind them. Rub on all surfaces of the chicken. Cover the pan tightly and refrigerate overnight.

In a heavy skillet, sauté the chicken over medium to high heat on all sides until well browned. When done, remove chicken and place in a small soup pot.

Onion, diced	1 lb.
Green bell pepper, chopped	8 oz.
Chicken stock	as needed

Using the same skillet, sauté the onions and pepper until just soft. Deglaze the skillet with a small amount of stock and transfer contents of skillet to the soup pot.

Chicken stock	2½ qt.
Salt and black pepper	to taste

Add the stock to the pot and bring to a boil. Lower heat, skim as needed, and simmer for 20 minutes or until the chicken is done. Add salt and pepper. Let cool, refrigerate, then skim fat. Reserve.

Yams, cut into 1-inch cubes	2 lb.

Cook yams in lightly salted water until just tender. Let cool and reserve.

Cilantro leaves, fresh, chopped	as needed

To prepare an individual serving: Reheat 6 oz. of the chicken soup with a piece of the cooked chicken. Add 2 oz. of the cooked yams and heat through. Serve with a sprinkling of fresh, chopped cilantro leaves.

CLAM AND MACKEREL SOUP   *Colombia*

Yield: 10–12 servings

Clams, small	5 doz.
Fish stock *or* water	1 pint

Scrub the clams; place in a soup pot with the fish stock, cover, and cook over high heat for 3–5 minutes, or until the clams open. Do not overcook or the clams will toughen. Remove the clams (leaving them in the shell) and reserve. Decant the clam broth and add enough fish stock or water to bring the quantity of liquid to 2 qt. Reserve.

Olive oil *or* vegetable oil	2 oz.
Bell pepper, seeded and chopped	2 lb.
Onion, small dice	1 lb.
Garlic, minced	1 tsp.

Rinse the pot and heat the oil over medium heat. Sauté the peppers and onions until soft. Add the garlic, stir well, and continue to cook for another minute.

Tomatoes, peeled, seeded, and diced	2 lb.
Potatoes, large dice	1½ lb.
Parsley, chopped	6 tbsp.
Bay leaf	2
Cumin, ground	½ tsp.

Add the tomatoes and cook for 2–3 minutes, then return the stock to the pot and bring to a boil. Add the potatoes, herbs, and seasonings and simmer for 10–15 minutes, or until the potatoes are tender. Let cool and reserve.

Mackerel fillets,* cut into 1-inch slices	2 lbs.
Parsley, fresh, chopped	as needed

To serve, reheat soup as needed. Add 2–3 oz. of mackerel per serving. When the fish is barely done, add 5–6 clams in the shell per serving and reheat. Pour into large, heated bowls and serve with a sprinkling of chopped fresh parsley.

---

*Any firm-fleshed fish can be substituted.

Serve as a luncheon entrée with croutons. If served as a first course adjust the quantity.

CHICKEN SOUP WITH FRESH CORN   *Mexico*

Yield: 10–12 servings

Chicken stock	3 qt.
Chicken breast, skinned, bone in	2 lb.
Onion, peeled and quartered	12 oz.
Celery, thick sliced	8 oz.
Carrot, small cubes	8 oz.
Coriander seeds	1 tsp.

Place the stock, chicken, vegetables, and coriander seeds in a small soup pot and bring to a boil. Lower heat and simmer for 20 minutes, skimming as necessary. When done, remove chicken breasts and take the meat from the bone. Shred the meat into strips and reserve. Remove the carrot cubes and reserve. Strain the broth, discard the remaining vegetables, degrease, and return the broth to a clean pot.

Corn, cut fresh off the cob	10 ears
Reserved broth	
Salt and black pepper	to taste

Just prior to serving, add the corn and salt and pepper to the broth and simmer for 5 minutes. Return the chicken and carrots to the pot. Let cool and reserve, refrigerated, until needed.

Tomatoes, peeled, seeded, and chopped *or* Salsa Cruda (see the recipe" in the "Salsas, Condiments, and Dressings" section)	as needed

Add 1 tbsp. of fresh tomatoes or Salsa per serving and heat through.

CHAYOTE SOUP   *Brazil*   Yield: 10–12 servings

Olive oil	2 oz.
Onion, small dice	1 lb.
Cucumber, peeled, seeded, then diced	1 lb.
Celery, strings peeled, cut into small dice	8 oz.

In a soup pot, heat the oil and sauté the onion over low heat until soft. Do not brown. Add the cucumber and celery, cover, and cook for 4–5 minutes.

Chicken stock	2½ qt.
Thyme	5–6 sprigs
Mint	5–6 sprigs
Parsley, flat	5–6 sprigs
Chili pepper, dried	1
Ginger root, minced	1 tsp.

Add the chicken stock. Tie the herbs, chili pepper, and ginger root in a double layer of cheesecloth for easy removal and add to the pot. Bring to a boil, lower heat, and simmer for 10 minutes.

Chayote, peeled, seeded, and chopped	3 lb.
Salt and white pepper	to taste
Nutmeg, grated	to taste
Sugar	to taste

Add the chayote and simmer for another 10–15 minutes, or until the chayote is tender. Remove the herbs and pepper and strain the liquid. Using a food processor, puree the vegetables. Return the vegetables to the stock and season with salt, white pepper, nutmeg, and sugar.

Serve hot, garnished with small sprigs of parsley or fresh mint leaves. If soup is to be served cold, increase the seasonings a bit and garnish with sour cream or unseasoned whipped cream.

TULI MACHI   *Panama*   Yield: 10 servings

Coconut milk, 50/50 thin and thick	2½ qt.
Banana, sliced in ¾-inch rounds	1 lb. (peeled weight)

In a small, heavy soup pot, bring the coconut milk to a boil. Lower heat to a simmer, then add the banana and cook until soft. Pass through a food mill. Reserve.

White fish and crab or lobster meat, cut in small pieces	2 – 3 oz. per serving	
Salt	to taste	
Tabasco sauce	to taste	
Lemon, quartered	as needed	

When ready to serve, reheat the soup as needed. Add a combined weight of 2 – 3 oz. of any firm-fleshed fillet of white fish and crab or lobster meat. Cook for 2 – 3 minutes, or until the fish flakes. Add salt and Tabasco sauce. Serve with lemon wedges on the side.

This dish is a specialty of the Indian region of San Blas in Panama.

TOMATILLO SOUP   *Mexico*

Yield: 10 – 12 servings

Olive oil	2 oz.
Onion, chopped	1½ lb.
Bell pepper, seeded and chopped	1 lb.
Celery, chopped	12 oz.
Sugar	1 tbsp.

In a heavy soup pot, heat the oil over medium heat. Add the vegetables, sprinkle lightly with sugar, and stir. Sauté, stirring occasionally, until the onions begin to get soft and color slightly.

Tomatillos, green, firm	3 ½ lb.
Jalapeños, seeded and chopped	2 whole
Ginger root, chopped	1 tbsp.
Mint, fresh, chopped	2 tbsp.
Thyme, dried	1 tbsp.
Parsley, flat	3 sprigs

Remove the papery husks from the tomatillos and wash. Cut them in half and add them to the pot, along with the jalapeños, ginger root, and herbs. Lower heat, cover, and cook for another 10 minutes.

Cucumbers, peeled, seeded, and chopped	4
Chicken stock	as needed
Salt and white pepper	to taste
Sugar	to taste

Add the cucumbers and enough chicken stock to make up 3 qt. Simmer for 20 minutes. When done, pass the contents of the pot through a food mill using the fine mesh strainer. Discard any pulp, seeds, and skins. Season with salt, white pepper, and sugar.

(Continued)

This soup may be served hot or cold. If served hot, garnish with chopped, fresh cilantro leaves. If served cold, a little more salt may be desired. Garnish with fresh mint or cilantro.

CONCH CHOWDER *Haiti*

Yield: 10–12 servings

Vegetable oil or bacon fat	2 oz.	Heat oil in a stainless steel or enameled soup pot over low to medium heat. Add the vegetables and cook, stirring occasionally, until they are soft, but not browned.
Onion, chopped	1 lb.	
Celery, chopped	4 stalks	
Garlic, minced	1 tbsp.	
Conch meat	2 lb.	Grind meat twice then add to the pot. Mix thoroughly with the vegetables and cook over low heat for 15 minutes.
Tomatoes, peeled and chopped	4 lb.	Add these ingredients and bring to a boil. Lower heat and simmer, partially covered for 45 minutes.
Chicken stock	16 oz.	
Tomato paste	2 tbsp.	
Oregano, dried	1 tbsp.	
Thyme, fresh leaves	1 tsp.	
Cayenne pepper	to taste	
Salt and pepper, black	to taste	
Potatoes, cubed	1½ lb.	Add the potatoes and carrots and simmer for another 10–15 minutes or until these vegetables are tender. Adjust seasonings, if necessary.
Carrots, cubed	½ lb.	
Sherry, dry	as needed	Serve in heated bowls with sherry and Tabasco sauce served on the side.
Tabasco sauce	as needed	

BEANS, RICE, AND OTHER STARCHES

RICE WITH CILANTRO AND POBLANO CHILIES   *Mexico*

Yield: 10–12 servings

Vegetable oil	4 oz.
Onion, minced	12 oz.
Rice, long grain	1 lb.

In a heavy saucepan, heat oil over moderate heat and sauté the onions until soft. Add the rice, mix well, and continue to cook, stirring occasionally, for another 2–3 minutes, until the oil is absorbed.

Poblano chilies, roasted, peeled, seeded, and ribs removed	3–4
Garlic, minced	2 tsp.
Cilantro leaves, fresh, chopped	1–2 bunches
Chicken stock	40 oz.
Salt	to taste

Puree the chilies, garlic, and cilantro in a food processor. Add a small amount of the chicken stock to make a smooth puree. Add this to the rice, along with the remainder of the stock. Mix well, cover, and simmer until all of the liquid has been absorbed and the rice is tender. Add salt.

MEXICAN-STYLE RICE

Yield: 10–12 servings

Corn oil	4 oz.
Rice, long grain	1 lb.

In a heavy saucepan, heat oil over moderate heat. Add the rice and sauté, stirring, until the rice begins to color.

Onion, small dice	1 lb.
Garlic, minced	1 tsp.

Add the onion and garlic and cook, over low heat, until the onion is soft.

Tomatoes, peeled and chopped	1½ lb.
Chicken stock	32 oz.

Add the tomato and mix well. Then add the chicken stock and bring to a boil. Stir, lower heat, and simmer, covered, until the rice is tender and all of the liquid has been absorbed.

Garnish each serving with a tablespoon of fresh, cooked peas.

BLACK BEAN SALAD   *Cuba*   Yield: 10–12 servings

Black beans	1½ lb.

Wash beans and remove any debris. Soak beans in water overnight. Discard the water and rinse beans well.

Water	3 qt.

Place beans in a stockpot with the water. Bring to a boil. Lower heat and simmer for 1½ hours or until the beans are tender. Do not overcook. Remove from heat and drain. Let cool and reserve.

Tomatoes, peeled, seeded, and chopped	2 lb.
Onion, red, sliced thin	½ lb.

When the beans have cooled add the tomato and onion.

Olive oil	12 oz.
Vinegar, wine	3 oz.
Dry mustard	1 tsp. or to taste
Chili sauce	1 tbsp.
Garlic, minced	1 tsp.

Combine the remaining ingredients and add to the beans. Mix gently and thoroughly, taking care not to mash the beans. Cover and refrigerate for several hours before serving.

BLACK BEAN PUREE   *Guatemala*   Yield: 10–12 servings

Black beans	1 lb.
Onion, chopped	8 oz.
Garlic, chopped	3 cloves
Black pepper	1 tsp.

Soak the beans in water overnight. Rinse well, then place beans in a soup pot with enough water to cover. Add the onion, garlic, and pepper. Cover and bring to a boil. Lower heat and simmer for 1½ hours, or until the beans are very tender. Add more water from time to time, if necessary. When done, place the beans in the bowl of a food processor fitted with a steel blade. Puree to a very smooth consistency. Reserve the bean puree in the processor.

Onions, sliced thin	8 oz.
Corn oil *or* lard	4 oz.
Salt and pepper	to taste

Fry the onions in the oil until brown and crisp. Add the oil to the bean puree and, using the pulse action, incorporate. Remove the puree to a mixing bowl and add the browned, crisp onions. Add salt and pepper.

Serve as an appetizer, or as a side dish for meat or poultry entrées.

BLACK BEANS   *Cuba*

Yield: 10–12 servings

Black beans	1½ lb.
Onion, whole	1 large
Salt pork, cut in cubes	6 oz.
Cilantro, fresh	10–12 sprigs
Bay leaf	2
Sugar	1 tsp.

Soak the beans overnight. Rinse well and place in a saucepan with enough cold water to cover to a depth of 3–4 inches above the level of the beans. Bring to a boil and let cook for 2–3 minutes. Drain water and begin the process once again, using boiling water and adding the onion, salt pork, herbs, and sugar. Simmer for 1 hour or more, or until the beans are very tender. If necessary, add water during the cooking process. Drain the beans and reserve about 8 oz. of the cooking liquid. Remove 1 cup of the beans and mash them. Mix the mashed beans with the reserved cooking liquid. Return the mashed, liquified beans to the pot along with the rest of the beans. Set aside.

Olive oil	2 oz.
Onion, chopped	1½ lb.
Green bell pepper, seeded and diced	1 lb.
Garlic, minced	2 tsp.

In a separate skillet, heat the oil over medium heat and sauté the onions and peppers. When soft, add the garlic and continue to cook for another minute.

Vinegar, wine	3 oz. or to taste
Sugar	2 tsp.

Add the vinegar and sugar to the skillet and bring to a boil. Remove from heat and add to the beans. Blend by stirring gently.

Serve with rice cooked with achiote oil. (Achiote oil — See "Regional Flavorings.")

BLACK BEANS AND RICE FLAVORED WITH RUM   *Cuba*

Yield: 10–12 servings

Black beans	1 lb.

Soak the beans overnight. Rinse well and reserve.

Olive oil	2 oz.
Onions, diced	1 lb.
Carrots, diced	8 oz.
Celery, diced	8 oz.
Garlic, minced	1 tbsp.

In a saucepan large enough to hold the beans, heat the oil over medium heat. Sauté the onions, carrots, and celery until soft. Add the garlic and cook for another minute.

Water	1½ qt.
Cilantro leaves, fresh, chopped	4 tbsp.
Salt	2 tsp.
Black pepper	1 tsp.

Add the water, cilantro, and pepper and bring to a boil. Cover pan, lower heat to simmer, and cook for an hour, or until the beans are tender. (Cooking time will vary.)

Rum, dark	2–3 oz. or to taste
Salt and black pepper	to taste

When done, add the rum, salt, and pepper, mix well, cover, and reserve in a warm place.

Water	40 oz.
Rice, long grain	1 lb.

In a separate saucepan, bring the water to a rapid boil. Add the rice, cover, and simmer for 20 minutes, or until the rice is tender. To serve, spoon beans over a bed of rice.

Serve hot and garnish with a sprinkling of chopped, fresh cilantro or parsley leaves. Serve as an entrée with a green salad. Use smaller portions if served as a side dish with meat, fish, or poultry entrées.

BEANS AND RICE   *Jamaica*   Yield: 10–12 servings

Coconut Milk:

Coconuts	2	Follow instructions for making undiluted or thick coconut milk (see the recipe in the "Regional Flavorings" section). When you have reached the point where the coconut pulp has been grated, line a bowl with a double layer of cheesecloth, then place the grated coconut in the center. Add the water several cups at a time and squeeze to extract the liquid. Repeat this process using all of the water. Reserve the coconut milk.
Water	1½ qt.	

Kidney beans	1 lb.	Soak beans overnight. Rinse well and place in a small soup pot with enough fresh water to cover. Add the celery and green pepper. Bring to a boil, then lower heat, cover, and simmer for ½ hour.
Celery ribs, each cut in half	4	
Green bell pepper, seeded and halved	1	

Thyme	1 tsp.	Add the reserved coconut milk and thyme. Simmer, stirring occasionally, for 45 minutes, or until the beans are tender.

Rice, white, long grain	1 lb.	Add the rice to the beans. Mix well, cover, and simmer for an additional 20 minutes. If needed, add additional water or coconut milk if the liquid is absorbed before the rice is done. When done, all the liquid will have been absorbed and the rice will be tender.

COUCOU   *Trinidad*   Yield: 10–12 servings

Okra, trimmed and sliced crosswise in ¼-inch rounds	1 lb.	Prepare the okra and set aside.

(Continued)

Water *or* beef stock	as needed
Salt	1 tsp.
Oregano	2 tsp.

Fill the bottom half of a double boiler with enough water to just reach the top half. Bring to a boil. Put the top section of the double boiler in place and fill with 2 qt. of boiling water or beef stock. Add the salt, oregano, and okra. Adjust heat to slow boil and cook for 5–6 minutes.

Cornmeal, white	14 oz.
Butter, sweet	4 oz.
Butter	as needed

Add the cornmeal in a slow, steady stream, stirring continuously. Cook for 5 minutes. Add the butter, stir well, cover, and cook over very low heat for another 10–15 minutes, stirring occasionally. When done, pour into a buttered glass or stainless-steel pan to mold. To serve, unmold, cut into slices, and reheat in butter.

Serve as a starch with meat or fish entrées, or as a light entrée garnished with boiled sweet potatoes, roasted sweet peppers, tomatoes, and olives.

FAROFA   *Brazil*

Yield: 10–12 servings

Butter, whole	8 oz.
Eggs, beaten	4
Farhina de manioca*	6–8 oz.
Salt	to taste

Heat the butter in a heavy skillet over medium heat until it foams. Add the eggs and cook as you would for scrambled eggs. When the eggs are still very loose, gradually add the farhina de manioca, stirring constantly, until the mixture has the consistency of coarse bread crumbs.

Serve as a starch with roasted meats or poultry.

Variations:
1. Add sautéed onions and parsley.
2. Add sautéed, grated carrots, and raisins.
3. Add cubed, soft white cheese to the beaten eggs.
4. Toast in a skillet over low heat or place in a shallow pan in a moderate oven, shaking frequently, until very light brown. Place in a shaker or serve from a small bowl to sprinkle on poultry, meats, and vegetables.

---

*Farhina de manioca is processed into flour from the root vegetable Cassava or Manioc. Pearl Tapioca is also made from this starch. Tapioca flour is used as a thickening agent and for making clear fruit glazes.

RICE WITH PINTO BEANS   *Cuba*

Yield: 10–12 servings

Pinto beans	¾ lb.

Place beans in enough cold water to cover to a depth of 1½ inches. Bring to a boil, then lower heat and simmer until the beans are tender but not too soft. Drain beans and reserve both beans and cooking liquid.

Salt pork *or* slab bacon, small dice	8 oz.
Achiote oil (see the recipe in the "Regional Flavorings" section)	2 tbsp.
Onion, diced	1 lb.
Garlic, minced	2 tbsp.
Tomatoes, peeled and chopped	2 lb.
Peppers, seeded and chopped	1 lb.
Black pepper	½ tsp.

In a heavy saucepan, sauté the salt pork or bacon in the achiote oil until the fat has been rendered. Add the onions and cook until soft. Add the garlic and cook for another minute. Add the tomatoes, peppers, and seasonings and cook over low heat for 5–6 minutes.

Rice, long grain	¾ lb.
Liquid	1 pt.
Capers	2 tbsp.

Add the rice and 1 pt. of liquid. You may use the reserved cooking liquid from the beans (if not sufficient add water), water, or ham stock. Add the capers. Mix well. Bring to a boil, then lower heat and cover. Simmer until most of the liquid has been absorbed, about 15–20 minutes. Add the beans and stir gently. Cover and continue to cook over very low heat for another 5 minutes, or until all of the liquid has been absorbed.

QUINOA   *Peru*

Yield: approximately 15 servings

Quinoa	1 lb.
Water	2 qt.

Rinse the quinoa several times before using, and place it in a saucepan with the water. Bring to a boil, then lower heat and simmer for 10–12 minutes, or until the grain is just tender. Pour the contents of the pan through a fine mesh strainer to drain. Transfer the cooked grain to a sheet pan covered with clean towels and spread to cool. Reheat as needed.

Quinoa may be served simply, with a butter or oil dressing, or, when cool, placed in a tightly sealed container and refrigerated until needed. A versatile starch, quinoa may be used to accompany meat, poultry, or fish entrées as a substitute for rice or potatoes. It may also be added to soups, stews, and salads. Finely cut vegetables such as carrots, red bell peppers, onions, and celery may be sautéed and combined with cooked quinoa. Flavorings for such a mixture might incude fresh herbs, grated ginger root, olive oil or butter, and salt and pepper.

QUINOA SALAD   *Peru:*

Yield: 12 servings

Dressing:

Olive oil	8 oz.
Lime *or* lemon juice, fresh squeezed	4 oz.
Jalapeño pepper, seeded, ribs removed, and minced	1
Capers	2 tsp.
Salt and white pepper	to taste

Combine the oil, juice, jalapeño, capers, and salt and pepper and whisk until thoroughly blended. Adjust oil or juice, if necessary, to achieve a good flavor balance. Reserve.

Quinoa, cooked, then cooled	1 lb.
Cucumbers, peeled, cut lengthwise, seeded, and sliced thin	1½ lb.
Tomatoes, peeled, seeded, and diced	1½ lb.
Mozzarella, fresh, very small dice	½ lb.
Parsley leaves, chopped	3 tbsp.
Mint leaves, fresh, chopped	3 tbsp.

Combine the remaining ingredients thoroughly. Cover and refrigerate until needed.

Boston lettuce *or* radicchio	as needed
Olives, black *or* green	as needed
Cornichon	as needed

To serve, place mixed salad as needed in a bowl and add dressing. Toss to mix well. Place a bed of lettuce on a chilled salad plate and top with a mound of the dressed salad. Garnish wih 2–3 olives and cornichon.

Serve as an appetizer or luncheon platter. Adjust portion size and garnishes accordingly.

RICE AND KIDNEY BEANS   *Jamaica*

Yield: 10–12 servings

Kidney beans, dried	1½ lb.
Garlic	3 cloves

Place the beans and garlic in a saucepan with enough water to cover. Bring to a boil, then lower heat and simmer for about 1 hour, or until the beans are tender. When done, drain, discard the garlic, and reserve.

(Continued)

Oil	1 tbsp.
Rice, long grain	12 oz.
Coconut milk, thin	24 oz.
Scallions, chopped	2
Hot pepper, fresh, green	1
Thyme	2 sprigs
Salt and white pepper	to taste

In a separate saucepan, heat the oil and sauté the rice over low heat until the oil has been absorbed. Add the remaining ingredients and simmer until the rice is done. Add water if rice has absorbed the liquid before becoming tender. When done, remove the hot pepper and thyme sprigs and discard. Drain the beans and combine with the rice.

Serve as an accompaniment with fish, poultry, or meat entrées.

SAVORY RICE WITH RAISINS   *Panama*

Yield: 10 servings

Butter, whole, sweet	2 oz.
Rice, long grain	1 lb.

In a heavy-bottomed saucepan, heat the butter over medium heat. When melted, add the rice and stir to coat evenly. Sauté the rice for 2–3 minutes, stirring occasionally.

Coconut milk, thin	40 oz. or as needed
Cinnamon stick	3-inch piece
Raisins	3 oz.
Salt	½ tsp.

Add the coconut milk, cinnamon stick, raisins, and salt. Stir well and bring to a boil. Cover pot with a tight-fitting lid and lower heat to a simmer. Cook until all of the liquid has been absorbed and the rice is tender. If rice has absorbed all of the liquid and is not yet tender, add a small amount of water and continue to cook over low heat.

Butter	2 oz.

Remove the cinnamon stick and add the butter.

Serve with meat and poultry entrées.

GUATEMALAN-STYLE RICE

Yield: 10–12 servings

Corn oil	2 oz.
Rice	1 lb.

In a heavy-bottomed saucepan, heat the oil over low heat and sauté the rice, stirring, until it begins to color slightly.

Onion, minced	4 oz.
Red bell pepper, minced	4 oz.
Carrot, small dice	4 oz.
Tomato, peeled and seeded	4 oz.
Garlic, minced	2 tsp.

Add the vegetables and garlic, stir well, cover, and cook for 3–4 minutes over very low heat, stirring occasionally.

Chicken stock	1¼ qt.

Add the stock and bring to a boil. Stir well, reduce heat to simmer, and cover. Cook for 15–20 minutes, or until all of the liquids have been absorbed and the rice is tender.

SAFFRON RICE WITH PEAS *Cuba*

Yield: 10–12 servings

Saffron	1 pinch
Chicken stock, warmed	8 oz.

Pulverize the saffron stigmas and place in warmed chicken stock. Allow to steep for 30 minutes or longer to extract flavor and color.

Olive oil	3 oz.
Onion, small dice	8 oz.
Garlic, minced	2 tsp.

In a heavy-bottomed saucepan, heat the olive oil over medium heat and sauté the onion until soft. Add the garlic and cook for another minute.

(Continued)

Chicken stock	1 qt.
Rice, long grain	1 lb.
Salt	1 tsp.

Add the reserved stock with saffron and chicken stock and bring to a boil. Add the rice and salt, then cover with a tight-fitting lid and lower heat. Simmer for 15 minutes or until the rice is tender.

Peas, fresh or frozen	12 oz.

Add peas and, if needed, a little stock. Stir gently to mix the peas with the rice. Cover and simmer for 5–10 minutes more.

BLACK BEANS BAKED WITH HONEY AND RUM   *Caribbean*

Yield: 10–12 servings

Black beans	1½ lb.

Wash the beans, remove all debris, and soak in water overnight. Rinse well and discard the water. Place the beans in a soup pot with enough fresh water to cover. Bring to a boil, then lower heat and simmer until the beans are just tender but not too soft. Drain and rinse well under cold water. Reserve.

Slab bacon, rind removed, small dice	8 oz.
Onion, small dice	1 lb.
Garlic, minced	2 tsp.

Sauté the bacon until the fat has been rendered. Remove the bacon bits and reserve. Discard all but 3 or 4 tbsp. of the bacon fat. Add onion and sauté over low heat until soft. Add the garlic and cook for another minute.

Cider vinegar	8 oz.
Honey	4 oz.
Rum, dark	4 oz.
Sugar, brown	4 tbsp.
Ginger, fresh, minced	2 tbsp.
Dry mustard	1 tbsp.
Clove, ground	½ tsp.
Cinnamon	½ tsp.
Black pepper	½ tsp.
Chicken stock	as needed
Salt	to taste

Add the remaining ingredients. Mix thoroughly until the sugar is completely dissolved.

Combine the vinegar/honey mixture and the cooked beans in a pot just large enough to hold them. Add chicken stock to barely cover and the reserved bacon bits. Mix gently so that the beans are not mashed. Cover with a tight-fitting lid and bake in a 250 degree F oven for 4–5 hours. If needed, add a small amount of chicken stock from time to time.

RICE IN COCONUT MILK WITH RAISINS   *Colombia*

Yield: 10–12 servings

Coconut milk, thin	40 oz.
Raisins, golden	6 oz.
Butter	2 oz.

Heat the coconut milk in a heavy saucepan. When very warm, but not boiling, add the raisins and the butter and cook for a few minutes, or until the raisins become plump.

Sugar	3 tbsp.
Butter	2 oz.
Salt	1 tsp.
Rice, long grain	1 lb.

Add the sugar, butter, and salt and stir well. Add the rice and bring to a boil. Cover the pan and cook over very low heat until all of the liquid has been absorbed and the rice is tender.

Serve as an accompaniment for meat dishes.

Fish and Seafood

BACALAO AU GRATIN   *Puerto Rico*

Yield: 10–12 servings

Salt cod, dried	3 lb.

Soak the cod for 24 hours, changing the water several times. When ready for use, remove all skin and bones. Break into bite-sized pieces and reserve under refrigeration.

Butter, whole	4 oz.
Onion, small dice	2 lb.
Garlic, minced	2 tsp.
Tomato paste	5 oz.
Flour	2 oz.

In a heavy saucepan, heat the butter over low heat and sauté the onion until it begins to brown lightly. Add the garlic and tomato paste and continue to cook for a few more minutes. Add the flour and incorporate it thoroughly. Cook for 3–4 minutes.

Fish stock *or* water	16 oz.
White wine, dry	8 oz.
Lemon juice, fresh squeezed	2 oz.
Bay leaf	2

Add stock or water, wine, lemon juice, and bay leaf and simmer until the sauce begins to thicken slightly. Reserve.

Parmesan cheese, grated	as needed
Olives, green, stuffed with pimiento, sliced thin	as needed
Parsley, fresh, chopped	as needed

To prepare an individual serving, place 4–5 oz. of the flaked cod fish on the bottom of an individual-serving, ovenproof dish. Cover with the reserved sauce and top with grated cheese. Place in a 425 degree F oven until heated through and the top is golden brown. Garnish with sliced olives and chopped parsley.

An attractive presentation can be made by piping mashed potatoes around the edge of the serving dish to create an attractive border, then baking.

CRAB CAKES WITH FRUIT RELISH   *Cuba*

Yield: 10–12 servings

Chutney:

Fruit juice (orange, pineapple, lemon, and lime)	1 pint
Sugar	8 oz.
Cider vinegar	8 oz.
Ginger, fresh, minced	2 tsp.
Allspice, ground	1 tsp.
Salt	to taste
Tabasco sauce	to taste

Create a good balance of flavors if using a combination of fruit juices, not too sweet or tart. Heat fruit juices and add the sugar, vinegar, and spices. Stir until the sugar and spices are completely dissolved.

Fruits, tropical (papaya, mango, and pineapple)	2 lb.
Onion, large dice	1 lb.
Red bell pepper, seeds and membranes removed, then finely chopped	1½ lb.

Papaya, mango, and pineapple may be used singly or in combination, peeled, seeded, and diced. Add the fruits, onion, and pepper to the fruit juice mixture. Bring to a boil, then lower heat and simmer for 45 minutes. Let cool, then refrigerate until needed.

Crab Cakes:

Mayonnaise	4–5 oz.
Eggs, beaten	2
Cilantro leaves, chopped fine	3 tbsp.
Dijon mustard	1 tbsp.
Cumin, ground	1 tsp.
Tabasco sauce	to taste
Salt and white pepper	to taste

Mix the mayonnaise, eggs, herbs, and seasonings thoroughly.

Crabmeat, cooked	2½ lb.
Bread crumbs	4 – 5 oz.
Cornmeal	as needed

Remove any cartilage from the crabmeat. Add the crabmeat and the bread crumbs to the mayonnaise mixture and combine thoroughly. Shape into small cakes ½-inch thick by 3 – 4 inches round (size may vary). Press in cornmeal on both sides and edges. Refrigerate until needed.

Butter, clarified	as needed

Over medium to high heat, sauté the crab cakes in clarified butter (4 oz. per serving) until golden brown on each side. Drain on paper or clean kitchen towels, then place on a warm plate and serve with the fruit relish on the side.

Garnish with lemon slices placed on a bed of salad greens.

STUFFED CRAB   *Mexico*

Yield: 10 servings

Olive oil	3 oz.
Onion, minced	12 oz.
Garlic, minced	2 tsp.

In a heavy skillet, heat oil over medium heat and sauté the onion until soft. Add the garlic, reduce heat to low, and cook for another minute.

Tomatoes, peeled and chopped	1½ lb.
White wine, dry	4 – 5 oz.
Green olives, stuffed with pimiento, sliced thin	20
Jalapeños, seeded and minced	3
Cilantro leaves, fresh, chopped	4 tbsp.
Salt and black pepper	to taste

Add the tomatoes, wine, olives, peppers, and cilantro and bring to a boil. Lower heat and simmer for 10 minutes. Add salt and pepper. Let cool completely.

(Continued)

Crabmeat, cooked	2½ lb.

Remove all traces of cartilage from the crabmeat. Combine with the other ingredients and divide equally among 10 individual-serving, ovenproof casseroles or large, cleaned crab shells. Cover with plastic wrap and refrigerate until needed.

Bread crumbs	as needed
Parmesan grated cheese	as needed
Butter, whole	as needed

To prepare an individual serving: Remove plastic wrap, sprinkle casserole with bread crumbs and grated cheese, and dot with butter. Let the casserole come to room temperature, then place it in a 400 degree F oven for 10–15 minutes, or until the top begins to brown.

Serve with green or white rice and a salad of assertive greens and citrus fruits.

DEVILED LOBSTER   *Caribbean*   Yield: 10–12 servings

Butter, clarified	as needed
Scallions, green and white parts, chopped	4
Onion, small dice	1½ lb.
Tomato, peeled, seeded, and chopped	2 lb.

Heat the clarified butter in a heavy skillet and sauté the scallions and onions until soft. Add the tomatoes and simmer for 15 minutes. Let cool and reserve.

Lobster meat, cooked, diced	2 lb.
Bread crumbs, toasted	5 oz.
Eggs, hard boiled and chopped fine	5

Combine the lobster meat, bread crumbs, and eggs and reserve.

Butter, whole	3 oz
Flour	2 oz.
Milk	16 oz.

Melt the butter and add the flour. Cook over low heat, stirring, for 3–4 minutes. Add the milk and, stirring constantly, bring to a boil. Lower heat and simmer until the milk begins to thicken.

Lime juice	3 oz.
Tabasco sauce	to taste
Salt and white pepper	to taste

Add the reserved tomato sauce and lobster to the milk. Mix well and add the lime juice, hot pepper sauce, and salt and pepper. Let mixture cool. Then spoon into individual ramekins or into large shells. Cover and refrigerate.

| Butter | as needed |

To serve: Dot with butter and bake in a 375 degree F oven until heated through and top begins to brown.

DOLPHIN FILLETS
St. Thomas

Yield: 10–12 servings

Marinade:

Lime *or* lemon juice, fresh squeezed	8 oz.
Corn oil	2 oz.
Black pepper	2 tsp.
Salt	1 tsp.

Combine the juice, oil, salt, and pepper and mix using a wire whisk until thoroughly blended.

| Dolphin fish, *or* other firm-fleshed, white fish, filleted | 4½–5 lb. |

Place the fish fillets in a single layer in a glass or stainless-steel pan and pour the marinade on top. Cover and refrigerate for at least 3 hours. Reserve until needed.

(Continued)

Sauce:

Corn oil	2 oz.
Onions, sliced thin	1 lb.
Garlic, minced	1 tbsp.
Italian peppers, sweet, seeds removed and diced fine	1 lb.
Tomatoes, peeled and chopped	3 lb.
Tomatillos, peeled and chopped	1½ lb.
Ginger root, minced	1 tbsp. or to taste
Tabasco sauce	to taste
Salt and black pepper	to taste

In a heavy saucepan, heat the oil and sauté the onions until soft. Add the garlic and Italian peppers and continue to sauté for another minute. Add the tomatoes, tomatillos, and seasonings and simmer, stirring occasionally, until the sauce has thickened. Adjust seasonings. Let cool, then refrigerate until needed.

Fish:

Flour	as needed
Oil	as needed

To prepare an individual serving: Dredge the fish in flour and fry in hot oil until crisp. Cover a deep, heated plate with a generous amount of the sauce. Place the fish fillet on top and garnish with thin slices of fresh lime.

Dolphin fish is found in the Caribbean. If unavailable, substitute any firm-fleshed white fish.

FISH BAKED WITH OLIVES AND SWEET PEPPERS   *Chile*

Yield: 10–12 servings

Sauce:

Red bell pepper, sweet	1 lb.

Roast peppers in a 450 degree F oven until the skins begin to char. Remove from heat, cover for five minutes, then remove the skins. Discard seeds and slice the peppers into very thin strips. Set aside.

Olive oil	1 oz.
Achiote oil	1 oz.
Onion, chopped	8 oz.
Cilantro leaves, fresh, chopped	10 sprigs
Olives stuffed with pimientos, coarsely chopped	4 oz.

In a heavy skillet, heat the oils over medium heat. Add the onion and sauté until soft. Add the cilantro and olives and continue to cook for another minute.

Orange juice, fresh or from concentrate	12 oz.
Lemon juice, fresh squeezed	4 oz. or to taste
Salt and white pepper	to taste

Add the citrus juices and simmer for 5 minutes. Add the roasted peppers and salt and pepper. Cool and reserve until needed.

Butter	as needed
Cod, snapper, *or* any white, firm-textured fish	6–8 oz. per serving

Lightly butter an ovenproof baking dish large enough to hold the desired number of fillets in a single layer. Cover with a light layer of the sauce. Bake, uncovered, in a 375 degree F oven for 10–15 minutes, or until the fish is done. To prepare a single serving use an individual-portion, ovenproof serving dish. Cooking time will vary, depending on the thickness of the fillet.

To serve, place the fish on a warm plate and spoon sauce on top. Garnish with finely chopped hard boiled eggs and sprigs of fresh cilantro or curly parsley.

This dish may also be prepared using whole fish such as porgie or croaker. For a single-portion serving, use fish weighing ¾–1 pound each.

MARINATED FISH ON A SKEWER   *Peru*

Yield: 10-12 servings

Marinade:

Garlic, peeled	5 medium cloves
Jalapeños, seeded, ribs removed	4
Vinegar, wine	12 oz.
Olive oil	4 oz.
Cumin, ground	1 tsp.
Salt and white pepper	to taste

Place garlic and peppers in a food processor and puree until smooth. With the motor running, add the vinegar, oil, and seasonings, and process for a minute or two until thoroughly combined.

Cod, swordfish, *or* any firm, white-fleshed fish cut into 1½-inch cubes	5 lb.

Trim fish and debone. In a glass or stainless-steel container, toss fish in the marinade. Cover and refrigerate for 4-6 hours.

To prepare an individual serving, place 6-8 oz. of fish on a skewer. Broil or grill 2-3 minutes on each side turning once. During cooking, baste with the marinade.

This marinade can be made in advance in larger quantities and kept in a tightly sealed jar in the refrigerator.

FISH FILLET CURAÇAO

Yield: 10–12 servings

Marinade:

Lime juice, fresh	8 oz.
Corn oil	4 oz.
Garlic, minced	1 tbsp.
Jalapeño, fresh, minced	1
Salt and black pepper, coarsely ground	to taste

Combine the lime juice, oil, garlic, pepper, and seasonings and mix well using a wire whisk. Reserve for later use in the sauce.

Snapper, turbot, *or* any other firm-fleshed white fish, filleted	4–5 lb.

Place the fish fillets in a glass or stainless-steel pan and cover all surfaces with the marinade. Cover and refrigerate for 3–4 hours. Reserve until needed.

Sauce:

Corn oil	2 oz.
Scallions, chopped, green and white parts	12
Red bell pepper, seeded and chopped	2
Tomatoes, peeled and chopped	4 lb.
Tabasco sauce	to taste
Salt and black pepper	to taste

Heat the oil in a heavy saucepan and sauté the scallions over medium heat. Add the red peppers, tomatoes, and seasonings to taste. Simmer until the sauce begins to thicken. Reserve.

(Continued)

Flour	as needed
Oil	as needed

To prepare an individual (6–8 oz.) serving: Cut the fish into pieces if the fillets are too large. Dredge in flour and fry quickly in hot oil until crisp. Transfer to an individual-serving, ovenproof dish. Mix the heated tomato sauce with a tablespoon or two of the marinade. Pour this mixture over the fish and place in a 400 degree F oven for 10–15 minutes, or until the fish is done. (Cooking time will vary depending on thickness of fillets.)

Serve with white rice.

GROUPER WITH TOMATO-BANANA SAUCE AND MANGO CHUTNEY *Jamaica*

Yield: 10–12 servings

Chutney:

Butter, whole	2 oz.
Onion, small dice	1 lb.
Curry powder	3 tbsp.
Mangoes, diced	2
Raisins	2 oz.
Applesauce	8 oz.
Heavy cream	6 oz.

Melt the butter over medium heat and sauté the onion until soft. Add the curry powder, mix well, and cook over low heat for about 5 minutes. Add the mangoes, raisins, and applesauce and simmer for 8–10 minutes. Let cool and reserve. When ready to serve add the heavy cream and reheat. This may be done for individual portions by reheating small amounts of the chutney with a generous splash of heavy cream.

Butter, clarified	as needed
Grouper, Mahi-Mahi, *or* other firm-fleshed, white fish	ten 8–10 oz. fillets
Flour	as needed

To prepare an individual serving: Heat the butter over moderate to high heat. Dredge the fish fillets in flour, shaking off any excess. Sauté for 2–3 minutes on each side, or until lightly browned. Remove fish to a warm plate.

Tomato, peeled, seeded, and chopped	as needed
Banana, sliced ½-inch thick	as needed
Tabasco sauce	to taste
Parsley sprigs	as needed

Place 3 – 4 tbsp. of the tomato along with 4 – 5 slices of banana in the skillet and tabasco sauce to taste. Cook, stirring for 1 – 2 minutes, or until heated through. Place sauce on top of the fillets and garnish with sprigs of fresh parsley.

Serve the mango chutney, warm, on the side.

BAKED SNAPPER   *Cuba*

Yield: 10 servings

Butter, softened	1 lb.
Garlic, minced	2 tbsp.
Cilantro leaves, fresh, chopped	6 tbsp.
Lemon juice, fresh squeezed	2 oz.
Salt and white pepper	to taste

Combine the butter, garlic, cilantro, lemon juice, and seasonings thoroughly and reserve.

Aluminum foil *or* parchment paper	10 pieces

Fold foil or paper in half. Each folded piece should be 2 inches larger on all sides than the fillet it will enclose.

Snapper fillets	ten 6 – 8-oz. fillets
Tomato, peeled and chopped	as needed
Onion, sliced very thin	as needed
Butter, melted	as needed

Spread some of the garlic-cilantro butter on the sheets of aluminum foil or parchment paper. Place one fish fillet in the center. Spread a bit more of the butter on top of the fillet. Place a layer of tomato and onion over the buttered fillet. Fold over to make a sealed packet. If using parchment paper, brush the outside of packet with melted butter. Refrigerate until needed.

(Continued)

Lemon wedges	as needed

To prepare an individual serving, place a packet containing the fish on a pan and bake in a 400 degree F oven for 15–20 minutes. (Cooking time will depend on the thickness of the fillet.) When done, the fish may be removed from the foil or paper and placed on a warmed plate. If served in the foil or paper, cut open the top of the packet to create an attractive, leaflike design, and place directly on a warm plate. Garnish with lemon wedges.

Serve with white or yellow rice.

GRILLED MARINATED TUNA   *Cuba*

Yield: 10 servings

Marinade:

Olive oil	6 oz.
Lemon juice, fresh squeezed	8 oz.
Garlic, minced	2 tbsp.
Shallot, minced	2 tsp.
Cumin, ground	1½ tsp.
Salt	1 tsp.
Black pepper	¾ tsp. or to taste
Cayenne pepper	to taste

Mix the oil, lemon juice, garlic, shallots, and seasonings.

Tuna fillets	ten 6–8-oz fillets
Cilantro leaves, fresh, chopped	2 bunches

Using a glass or stainless-steel container, arrange the tuna fillets in a single layer and pour the marinade on top. Turn the fillets once to coat the other side. Sprinkle the chopped cilantro evenly over the fillets. Cover and refrigerate for 4 hours or overnight.

Lemon wedges	as needed
Cilantro	as needed

To prepare an individual serving, remove fillet from the marinade, pat dry, and broil or grill over coals until done as desired. Garnish with lemon wedges and sprigs of fresh cilantro.

Serve with black bean salad.

FISH FILLETS PICKLED IN LIME AND VINEGAR   *Mexico*

Yield: 10–12 servings

Corn oil	8 oz.
Fish fillets, (any firm-fleshed, white fish)	5 lb.
Limes, sliced thin	as needed

Heat oil in a heavy skillet and sauté the fish over medium heat until lightly browned on both sides. Place the fish in a single layer in a glass or stainless-steel pan. Cover the fish with the lime slices and set aside.

Onion, red, thin sliced	1½ lb.
Garlic, minced	1 tbsp.
Jalapeños, roasted, peeled, seeded, deveined, and chopped fine	3

Using the same pan, sauté the onion rings, garlic, and jalapeños until the onion begins to soften, about a minute or so. Distribute these ingredients evenly over the fish and lime slices.

Vinegar, red wine	12 oz.
Oregano	1 tsp.
Salt	½ tsp.
Black pepper	½ tsp.

Using the same pan, bring the vinegar, oregano, salt, and pepper to a boil. Pour over the fish. Cover and refrigerate for several days before serving.

Drain each portion of the marinated fish when serving. Garnish with the pickled vegetables over a bed of lettuce as a luncheon dish, or serve bite-sized portions of the fish alone on croutons as an hors d'oeuvre.

SHRIMP CURRY   *Caribbean*   Yield: 10–12 servings

Curry Sauce:

Butter, whole	8 oz.
Onion, small dice	1½ lb.
Chayote, peeled and chopped	12 oz.
Garlic, minced	1 tsp.
Curry powder	1–2 tbsp. or to taste

In a heavy saucepan, melt the butter and sauté the onion over low heat until soft. Add the chayote, garlic, and curry powder and continue to cook for several minutes more.

Flour	3 oz.
Chicken stock	1 qt.
Tomato, seeded, peeled, and chopped	1½ lb.
Lime juice, fresh squeezed	2 oz.
Bay leaf	2
Ginger, fresh, minced	1 tsp.
Black pepper coarsely ground	to taste
Salt	to taste

Add the flour and incorporate thoroughly. Cook over low heat for 3–4 minutes, then add the stock, tomato, lime juice, and seasonings. Mix well and bring to a boil. Lower heat and simmer for 20–30 minutes. Adjust seasoning if necessary. Let cool and reserve. Sauce may be refrigerated until needed.

Shrimp, peeled and deveined	4–5 lb.

Prepare shrimp and place in a glass or stainless-steel container until needed. To prepare an individual serving: Put 4–5 oz. of the sauce in a small sauté pan and bring to a boil. Add 5–6 oz. of the shrimp and cook briefly over medium heat until the shrimp turn pink. Do not overcook.

Serve on a bed of warm white rice with mango or other fruit chutney served alongside.

SHRIMP, RICE, AND TOMATOES   *Caribbean*

Yield: 10 servings

Rice:

Slab bacon, diced	4 oz.	In a heavy saucepan, sauté the bacon until crisp. Reserve.

Onion, small dice	1½ lb.	Discard the excess fat in the pan and sauté the onion until soft. Add the garlic and hot peppers and continue to cook for another minute.
Garlic, minced	2 tsp.	
Hot peppers, fresh, seeded, and minced	1 tbsp. or to taste	

Rice, long grain	1 lb.	Add the rice and cook, stirring, until the grains are well coated. Add the chicken stock and tomatoes, stir well, and simmer, covered, until the rice is tender. Add salt and pepper and reserve.
Chicken stock	1 qt.	
Tomatoes, peeled, seeded, and chopped	3 lb.	
Salt and black pepper	to taste	

Shrimp, peeled, deveined, and butterflied	5 lb.	To prepare an individual serving: Over high heat, sauté the shrimp in clarified butter until they just turn pink. Add the chopped parsley and the cooked rice–tomato mixture, stir well, cover, and heat through.
Butter, clarified	as needed	
Parsley, chopped	1 tbsp.	

A good dish for buffet service. Add a small amount of chicken stock to the cooked rice. Then place rice, covered, in a 350-degree-F oven until heated through. Sauté shrimp just prior to serving, then add to heated rice. Mix thoroughly.

SHRIMP WITH BLACK BEAN SAUCE   *Caribbean*

Yield: 10–12 servings

Sauce:

Butter	4 oz.
Red bell peppers, seeds and membrane removed, chopped fine	2 lb.
Garlic, minced	1 tbsp.
Ginger root, minced	1 tbsp.

In a heavy skillet, heat butter over low to medium heat and sauté the peppers. When they have become soft, add the garlic and ginger root and continue to cook for another 2–3 minutes.

White wine, dry	24 oz.
Chicken stock	8 oz.
Salt and black pepper	to taste

Add the wine, stock, and seasonings and simmer for 10 minutes.

Black beans, cooked and mashed	10 oz.
Salt and pepper	to taste

Add the beans and mix well. Simmer, stirring occasionally, for 10–15 minutes. Adjust for salt and pepper. Let cool and reserve.

Shrimp, raw, large, peeled, and deveined	5–6 oz. per serving

Prepare shrimp by poaching in water or a court bouillon, or sautéing in oil over high heat. Place a pool of reheated black bean sauce on a warm plate. Arrange the cooked shrimp in an attractive circular pattern on top of the sauce.

Garnish with chopped, fresh coriander leaves. Accompany with fried plantains served on a separate plate.

BAKED SNAPPER WITH ALMONDS AND LIME   *Caribbean*

Yield: 1 serving

Whole fish (red snapper, porgy, croaker, *or* any firm-fleshed fillet)	¾ lb.
Flour	as needed
Butter, clarified	as needed

If using a whole fish, trim fins, remove all scales and gills, and wash thoroughly. Dust fish lightly with flour and sauté in clarified butter over medium to high heat until lightly browned on each side.

Butter, whole	1 tsp.
Almonds, toasted and chopped fine	2 tbsp.
Fish stock	4 oz.
Lime juice	2 tbsp.
Cilantro leaves, fresh chopped	1 tbsp.
Salt and white pepper	to taste
Lime, thinly sliced	as needed
Cilantro sprigs	as needed

Discard any excess clarified butter. Add the whole butter, almonds, stock, lime juice, and cilantro. Cover pan and place in a 375 degree F oven for 10–15 minutes, or until the fish flakes. (Cooking time will vary depending on thickness of fish.) When done, place fish on a warm plate. Reduce the pan juices over high heat. Add salt and pepper and garnish with thin slices of fresh lime and a few sprigs of cilantro.

RED SNAPPER IN ORANGE SAUCE   *Caribbean*

Yield: 1 serving

Butter, clarified	1 tbsp.
Onion, minced	2 tbsp.
Garlic, minced	½ tsp.
Orange juice, fresh	4 oz.
Cinnamon, ground	pinch
White pepper	to taste

Heat the butter in a skillet large enough to hold a 6–8-oz. fish fillet. Sauté the onion until soft. Add the garlic, orange juice, cinnamon, and white pepper. Simmer for another minute.

(Continued)

Snapper	one 8-oz. fillet
Green olives stuffed with pimiento, sliced	4 – 5

Place fish fillet in pan. Spoon some of the sauce on top. Arrange the sliced olives on top of the fish. Cover with aluminum foil and bake in a 400 degree F oven for 8 – 12 minutes or until the fish is done (Cooking time will vary depending on the thickness of the fillet.)

Cilantro, fresh, chopped	as needed
Orange, sliced	as needed

Place fish on a warm plate and garnish with fresh, chopped cilantro and slices of fresh orange.

AVOCADOS STUFFED WITH CRAB   *Cuba*

Yield: 10 servings

Avocados	10
Lemon *or* lime juice	as needed

Cut avocados in half and remove the pits. Using a small spoon, remove most of the avocado pulp, leaving a uniform ¼ inch of the pulp as a lining for the shell. Rub all cut surfaces with fresh lemon or lime juice to prevent discoloration. Reserve.

Lime juice, fresh squeezed	3 oz.

Place the avocado pulp in a glass or stainless-steel mixing bowl with the lime juice and mash to a very smooth consistency.

Scallions, white and tender green parts, chopped fine	10
Onion, minced	12 oz.
Parsley, fresh chopped	6 tbsp.
Garlic, minced	3 tsp. or to taste
Hot pepper, fresh, green, chopped fine	3 tsp. or to taste
Olive oil	2 oz.
Salt and black pepper, coarsely ground	to taste

Add the remaining ingredients except for the crabmeat and mix well.

Crabmeat, cooked	2 lb.

Remove any cartilage from the crabmeat. Using a fork and tossing lightly to avoid mashing the crabmeat, blend the crabmeat with the mashed avocado mixture. Fill the reserved shells to overflowing and refrigerate until needed.

As a luncheon entrée, serve two avocado halves on a bed of crisp greens garnished with roasted red peppers, other salad vegetables, and wedges of fresh lime. If served as an appetizer, use only one avocado half.

STUFFED CRABS
French Caribbean

Yield: 10 servings

Crabmeat, cooked	2½ lb.
Lime juice	2 oz.
Bread crumbs, toasted	10 oz.

Pick over the crabmeat and discard any bits of shell or cartilage. In a glass or stainless-steel bowl combine with lime juice and bread crumbs.

Hot pepper, seeds and ribs removed and minced fine	1 large
Rum, dark	4 oz.
Olive oil	2 oz.
Garlic, minced	2 tsp.
Parsley, fresh chopped	3 tbsp.
Allspice, ground	to taste
Salt	to taste

Add the hot pepper, rum, oil, garlic, parsley, and seasonings and mix well.

(Continued)

Bread crumbs	as needed
Butter, whole	as needed

Fill 10 large scallop shells or ramekins with the mixture, cover, and refrigerate.

To prepare an individual serving: Lightly sprinkle the filled shell with bread crumbs and dot with whole butter. Place in a 400 degree F oven until heated through and the top begins to brown slightly.

Makes a good luncheon dish accompanied by a salad of mixed greens tossed with a light oil-and-lemon dressing.

STUFFED SHRIMP
Dominican Republic

Yield: 10 servings

Stuffing:

Anchovy fillets	6–7
Butter	10 oz.
Onion, grated	2 oz.
Lime juice, fresh squeezed	2 oz.
White pepper	1 tsp.

Place the anchovy fillets, butter, onion, lime juice, and white pepper in the bowl of a food processor and, using the pulse action, blend thoroughly.

Bread crumbs, toasted	as needed

Add enough bread crumbs to the butter-anchovy mixture to make a fairly dry, but not crumbly, mixture.

Shrimp, jumbo	40 (16–20 count)
Lime juice, fresh squeezed	as needed

Peel and devein the shrimp. Deepen the incision to create a pocket for the stuffing. Stuff each shrimp with a generous teaspoonful of the anchovy mixture. Press the stuffing into the shrimp and smooth the surface. Arrange the shrimp in a glass or stainless-steel tray. Sprinkle with lime juice, cover, and refrigerate until needed.

Batter:

Flour, all-purpose	8 oz.
Beer	8 oz.
Vegetable oil	2 oz.
Eggs, separated	2
Salt	2 tsp.

Mix the flour, beer, oil, and egg yolks until batter is smooth. Beat the egg whites until stiff, then fold into the batter. The batter should have the consistency of a light pancake batter. Adjust with the addition of flour or beer if needed.

Flour	as needed

To prepare an individual serving: Dust the stuffed shrimp with flour. Coat with batter and deep-fry in oil at 375 degrees F.

Serve with Salsa Cruda (see the recipe in the "Salsas, Condiments, and Dressings" section) and lime wedges.

POMPANO WITH SHRIMP SAUCE *Cuba*

Yield: 10–12 servings

Shrimp Sauce:

Shrimp, cleaned, cooked, and chopped	2 lb.

Prepare the shrimp and reserve.

Butter, whole, sweet	3 oz.
Flour	4 oz.
Fish stock	20 oz.
Heavy cream	24 oz.
Sherry	to taste

In a heavy saucepan, heat the butter over medium heat until melted. Add the flour and mix well. Cook over low heat for 5–6 minutes, stirring occasionally, to make a smooth roux. Add the fish stock and the heavy cream. Using a wire whisk, blend these ingredients thoroughly. Add the sherry and simmer, stirring frequently, for 10 minutes.

Egg yolks, beaten with 1 tbsp. of water	5
Salt and white pepper	to taste

Beat the egg yolks in a separate bowl. Add a very small amount of the hot sauce to the yolks and mix with a wire whisk. Gradually add more of the sauce until the eggs are tempered.

(Continued)

Return this mixture to the remaining sauce. Mix well. Add the reserved shrimp, salt, and pepper. The sauce may be kept warm in a *bain marie* or cooled and reheated as needed. If reheating, heat the sauce to just below the boiling point prior to serving.

Pompano, red fish, *or* snapper	10–12 6-oz fillets
White wine	as needed
Butter, melted	as needed
Paprika, Spanish	as needed

To prepare an individual serving: Place a fish fillet in a small broiling pan with 2–3 oz. of white wine. Brush top of fillet with melted butter and broil until done. Place a pool of shrimp sauce on a warm plate, then arrange the fillet on top. Dust with a sprinkling of paprika.

Serve with yellow rice and peas.

FISH FILLETS "ESCABECHE"— THREE VERSIONS

Yield: 10 servings

Version 1—Peru:

Fish fillets (snapper, bass, cod, halibut, *or* any other firm-fleshed, white fish)	ten 7–8 oz. fillets
Flour	as needed
Salt and black pepper	to taste
Cayenne pepper	to taste
Oil, for deep-frying	as needed

Trim the fish and remove all bones. Dredge the fillets in a mixture of flour, salt, pepper, and cayenne and shake before frying to remove excess flour. Heat the oil to 350 degrees F and deep-fry until the fish is a light golden color. Remove with a skimmer or slotted spoon. Place the fish in a single layer in a glass or stainless-steel pan.

Oil, olive *or* vegetable	2 – 3 oz.
Onions, sliced thick	1½ lb.
Jalapeños, seeded and cut in thin strips	2 – 3 or to taste
Oregano	1 tbsp.
Vinegar, wine	24 oz.

In a skillet, heat the oil over medium heat and sauté the onions until they begin to color slightly. Add the jalapeños, and oregano and continue to cook for another 2 minutes. Add the vinegar, stir well, and simmer for 20 minutes. Pour the sauce over the fish, cover, and reserve. Serve at room temperature.

Version 2 — Peru:

Fish fillets (see above)	ten 7 – 8 oz. fillets
Flour	as needed
Paprika	to taste
Salt and black pepper	to taste

Trim the fish and remove all bones. Add paprika to the dredging mixture. Eliminate the cayenne. Follow method for Version 1.

Oil, olive or vegetable	4 oz.
Garlic, whole cloves	15

In a sauté pan, heat the oil over low to medium heat. Sauté the garlic until it just begins to color. Remove from the oil and reserve.

Jalapeños, seeded and sliced	4
Paprika	1 tbsp.
Fish stock	16 oz.
Red wine, dry	8 oz.
Vinegar, red wine	4 oz.
Cilantro sprigs	10
Salt	to taste

In the same pan, add the jalapeños and paprika and cook for another minute over low heat. Add the fish stock, wine, vinegar, cilantro, and salt and bring to a boil. Lower heat and simmer for 20 minutes. Pour immediately over the fried fish fillets. Distribute the garlic cloves over the fish. Cover, let cool, and serve at room temperature.

Version 3 — Mexico:

Fish fillets (see above)	ten 7 – 8 oz. fillets
Lemon juice	4 oz.
Oil, olive or vegetable	4 oz.

Trim the fish and remove all bones. Place the fish fillets in a glass or stainless-steel pan and toss in lemon juice. Let marinate in the refrigerator for 2 – 3 hours. Pat dry, then sauté in oil on both sides until lightly colored. Return the fillets to the same pan in which they were marinated, reserving the marinade separately.

(Continued)

Vinegar, white	16 oz.
Scallions, white and green parts, chopped	12
Serrano chilies, whole	2
Oregano	1 tbsp.
Garlic, minced	2 tsp.
Cinnamon stick	3 inch
Cloves	1 tsp.
Cumin, ground	1 tsp.
Salt and black pepper	to taste

In the same pan in which the fish was sautéed, add the remaining ingredients plus the reserved marinade and bring to a boil. Lower heat and simmer for 20 minutes. Pour over fish, let cool, and serve at room temperature.

Other flavored vinegars, herbs, and fish may be substituted when preparing these recipes.

Serve as a main course, or in smaller portions as an appetizer, especially as a warm-weather dish. Serve on a bed of shredded lettuce and garnish with thick slices of corn on the cob, green, pimiento-stuffed or black olives, hard boiled eggs, capers, radishes, and other garden vegetables. Tightly covered, escabeche can be stored in the refrigerator for 4–5 days.

SHRIMP "ESCABECHE"   *Peru*   Yield: 10–12 servings

Peanut oil	6 oz.
Shrimp, large, peeled and deveined, tail end of shell left on	4–5 lb. (21–25 count)

Heat the oil over high heat in a heavy skillet. Fry the shrimp quickly in small batches. Remove the shrimp as soon as they begin to turn pink and place them in a deep glass or stainless-steel bowl. Do not overcook.

Garlic cloves, peeled	6–8
Chili peppers, red, dried	4

Using the same pan, turn down the heat to low. Add the garlic and chili peppers. Sauté slowly until the garlic turns golden; do not let the garlic brown. Mash the cloves to extract flavor, then discard both the garlic and peppers.

Paprika, Spanish	1 tbsp.
Vinegar, white wine	16 oz.
White wine, dry	16 oz.
Rosemary *or* thyme, fresh	4–5 sprigs or to taste
Bay leaf	2

Using the same skillet, add the paprika. Cook for 20–30 seconds, stirring constantly. Add the remaining ingredients, raise heat to high, and bring to a boil. Lower heat and simmer for 10–15 minutes. Let liquid cool slightly, then pour over the shrimp. When cool, remove bay leaf, cover, and refrigerate.

Serve on a bed of lettuce and garnish with thick slices of corn on the cob, green, pimiento-stuffed or black olives, chopped parsley, and white, soft cheese.

SOFTSHELL CRABS IN TOMATO SAUCE   *Brazil*

Yield: 10–12 servings

Tomato Sauce:

Olive oil	2 oz.
Onion, small dice	1 lb.
Red peppers, fresh, hot, seeded and chopped	3 or to taste
Tomatoes, peeled, seeded, and chopped	3–3½ lb.
Cilantro leaves, fresh, chopped	4–5 tbsp.
Lime juice, fresh squeezed	2 oz. or to taste
Salt and black pepper	to taste

In a heavy saucepan, heat the oil over medium heat and sauté the onion until soft. Add the hot peppers and cook for another minute. Add the tomatoes, cilantro, lime juice, and salt and pepper and simmer for 20 minutes. Let cool and reserve.

Oil	as needed
Softshell crabs	2–3 per serving

Wash and dry the crabs. In a small sauté pan, heat a small amount of oil over medium-high heat and sauté the crabs for a minute on each side. Add 3–4 oz. of the reserved tomato sauce, lower the heat, cover, and cook for another 4–5 minutes, or until the crabs are done.

To serve, place the crabs on a bed of white rice and spoon the sauce on top. Garnish with wedges of fresh lime.

BAKED FISH FILLET WITH TANGERINE   *Brazil*

Yield: 10 servings

Snapper *or* bass, filleted	ten 6–8 oz. fillets
Lemon juice, fresh squeezed	as needed
Scallions, chopped, white and green parts	10–12
Salt and white pepper	to taste

Trim and remove all bones. Place the fillets in a single layer in a glass or stainless-steel pan. Add enough lemon juice just to cover. Distribute the scallions evenly over the surface of fish, then sprinkle lightly with salt and pepper. Marinate, covered, 3–4 hours in the refrigerator.

Butter	2 oz.
Olive oil	2 oz.
Mushrooms, sliced thin	1½ lb.

Heat the butter and oil over medium-high heat and sauté the mushrooms. When done, remove from the pan, let cool, and reserve.

White wine, dry	2 oz. per serving
Tangerine juice	1 oz. per serving
Parsley leaves, fresh, chopped fine	as needed

To prepare an individual serving: Place one fish fillet in an individual-portion, ovenproof serving dish along with several tablespoons of the marinade. Cover the top of the fillet with the mushrooms and add the white wine and tangerine juice. Cover with aluminum foil and bake in a 400 degree F oven for 8–10 minutes, or until the fish flakes easily. (Cooking time will vary depending on the thickness of the fillet.) Garnish with chopped, fresh parsley.

SHRIMP IN COCONUT SAUCE   *Caribbean*

Yield: 10–12 servings

Jalapeños *or* other chilies, seeded and chopped	3
Onions, sliced	1 lb.
Lemon zest	2 lemons
Ginger root, peeled and sliced	2-inch piece
Achiote oil*	2 tbsp.

Place the jalapeños, onions, ginger, and oil into the bowl of a food processor fitted with a steel blade. Puree to a smooth consistency.

Water	12 oz.

Add the water and pulse a few times. Transfer the contents of the processor bowl to a heavy saucepan.

Coconut milk*	24 oz.

Add the coconut milk to saucepan and heat, just under a boil, for 5 minutes, stirring. Let cool and reserve.

Shrimp, jumbo, peeled and deveined	4–5 oz. per serving
Scallion	as needed
Lemon juice, fresh squeezed	as needed

To serve, place 4–5 oz. of the reserved sauce in a small skillet. Heat just under a boil. Add the shrimp and cook until they are no longer translucent. Do not allow to boil. Garnish with thin strips of the tender green parts of the scallion and a few drops of fresh lemon juice.

---

*See the recipes in the "Regional Flavorings" section.

YUCA AND SALT COD SALAD   *Panama*

Yield: 10–12 servings

Salt cod	2½ lb.
Water	as needed

Soak the cod for 24 hours, changing the water several times. When ready to cook, place the fish in a saucepan and cover with water. Bring to a boil, then lower the heat and simmer for 10–15 minutes. Remove the fish and let cool. Discard any skin or bones, and then flake the fish and reserve.

Yuca, peeled	3 lb.
Water	as needed

Scrub the yuca, (also known as cassava), then cut into 2–3 inch round sections. Using a paring knife cut an incision into the outer bark deep enough to reach the underlayer. Place the paring knife beneath the underlayer to separate the peel from the usable portion of the tuber. Cut into ½-inch cubes. Place in cold water to cover to a depth of two inches and bring to a boil. Lower heat and simmer until all pieces can be pierced easily. As pieces become tender, remove from heat, let cool and reserve.

Reserved cod	
Reserved yuca	
Peppers, red roasted, peeled and cut julienne	1 lb.
Parsley, flat, chopped	4 tbsp.
Garlic, minced	2 tsp.
Oil, corn *or* olive	4 oz.
Vinegar, red wine	1 oz.
Salt and coarsely, crushed white peppercorns	to taste

Combine these ingredients and mix well. Refrigerate for several hours before serving.

Serve on lettuce leaf garnished with seasonal vegetables.

FRIED WHOLE FISH WITH PICKLED ONIONS AND LIME   *Mexico*

Yield: 1 serving

Whole fish; porgy; croaker; trout; eviscerated	¾ to 1 lb. each
Salt and black pepper	as needed
Cilantro	2 sprigs
Flour	as needed

Clean fish, removing all scales, gills, and fins. Trim tail fin; leave head on. Score each side of the fish with three diagonal cuts. Sprinkle lightly with salt and pepper and place the cilantro sprigs in the belly cavity. Dredge fish in flour. Shake to remove excess flour.

Oil, corn	as needed
Garlic, sliced	1 large clove
Reserved garlic, chopped	

Heat oil ½ inch deep in a skillet just large enough to hold the fish. Over low to medium heat, fry the garlic until it begins to brown lightly. Remove garlic and reserve. Do not let the garlic brown. Place fish in garlic flavored oil and fry until browned with crisp skin on one side. Turn fish and fry the other side. When done, place fish on a warm plate. Garnish with thin slices of red onions that have been marinated in lime juice and oregano and a sprinkling of capers. Sprinkle the sliced garlic on top.

Serve with chilled, steamed green beans and boiled potatoes dressed with oil and vinegar. Garnish plate with lime wedges. Serve salsa cruda on the side.

CHICKEN

JERK CHICKEN   *Jamaica*

Yield: 10 servings

Chickens, broiler	five 2¼-lb. birds
Jerk Marinade (see the recipe in the "Regional Flavorings" section)	approximately 2 cups
Water	as needed

Split each chicken in half and trim excess fat and skin. Place in a deep pan and immerse chicken in Jerk Marinade and a little water. Cover and refrigerate overnight, turning pieces occasionally.

Traditionally grilled over a slow fire containing the wood from the allspice tree, this preparation can be grilled over other aromatic woods such as apple or hickory. If this method is not practical, bake chicken in a 350 degree F oven for 30 minutes, basting twice with the marinade. Complete cooking over hot coals or under the broiler.

Use the same marinade for Cornish hens, chicken breasts, and chicken wings. Adjust cooking time if using these products.

DUCK BREAST WITH YAM AND MANGO   *St. Martin*

Yield: 10 servings

Duck:

Duck breasts,* singles	ten 10–12-oz. breasts
Rum, dark	6 oz.
Thyme, dried	2 tbsp.
Allspice, ground	2 tsp.
Salt	1 tsp.

Remove the skin and reserve. Marinate the duck in rum and seasonings over night. Sauté the reserved duck skins fat side down over medium heat until crisp. Cut into thin strips and reserve.

Sauce:

Vegetable oil	4 oz.
Shallots, minced	8 oz.
Scallions, white and green parts, chopped	8 oz.
Garlic, minced	1 tbsp.
Jalapeño, seeded, ribs removed, and minced	1 tsp. or to taste

In a heavy saucepan, heat the oil over moderate heat and sauté the shallots and scallions until soft. Add the garlic and jalapeño and continue to cook over low heat for another 5 minutes.

(Continued)

---

*Barberie duck.

Mango, green, peeled and cubed	2 lb.
White wine, dry	8 oz.
Salt and pepper	to taste
Sugar	to taste

Add the mango, white wine, salt, pepper, and sugar. Simmer until some of the liquid has evaporated and the sauce begins to thicken. Let cool and reserve.

To prepare an individual serving: Grill or sauté duck breast until done as desired (medium rare is best). Reheat sauce. Place a pool of the mango sauce on a warm plate. Slice breast meat on the diagonal and place, fanned out, on top of the sauce. Garnish with thin strips of the crisp duck skin.

Serve with slices of batata, or white yam, that have been boiled in lightly salted water and dressed with melted butter.

SPICY CHICKEN IN WALNUT SAUCE   *Peru*

Yield: 10–12 servings

Chickens, split, bone in, skin on	three 2½-lb. birds
Water	as needed
Onion, quartered	1 large
Carrot, large rounds	8 oz.
Celery	3 ribs

Place the chickens in a soup pot with enough water to cover. Bring to a boil, then lower heat and simmer for 20 minutes, skimming as necessary. Add the remaining ingredients and simmer for another 30–40 minutes, or until the chicken is cooked through and tender. Remove from heat and let chicken cool in the broth.

When cool enough to handle, pull the chicken meat from the bones. Discard the skin and bones. Chop the meat into slightly smaller than bite-sized pieces. Strain and degrease the stock. Discard the vegetables, then reserve the chicken and stock separately.

Olive oil	4 oz.
Onions, chopped	1½ lb.
Garlic, minced	2 tsp.
Chili pepper, hot, dried	1

Using a skillet large enough to hold the reserved chicken, heat the oil over medium heat and sauté the onion until soft. Add the garlic and cook for another minute. Add 1 pt. of the reserved stock and the chili pepper. Simmer until the liquid has been reduced by a third. Remove the chili pepper and discard.

Bread crumbs, white, fresh	8 oz.
Heavy cream	12 oz.
Parmesan cheese, grated	2 oz.
Walnuts, chopped fine	4 oz.
Cayenne pepper (optional)	to taste
Salt and white pepper	to taste

Gradually add the bread crumbs, stirring to incorporate thoroughly. Add the remaining ingredients and mix well.

Add the chicken and mix well. Adjust consistency with additional chicken stock, if necessary. Simmer for 5 minutes, let cool, and reserve. Heat through as needed.

Serve with potatoes, hard boiled eggs, and green, pimiento-stuffed olives.

CHICKEN WITH A BITTER ORANGE GLAZE *Cuba*

Yield: 10 servings

Marinade:

White wine, dry	8 oz.
Honey	6 oz.
Bitter orange* juice	6 oz.
Parsley, chopped	6 tbsp.
Mustard powder	2 tsp.
Salt	1 tsp.
Pepper	½ tsp.

In a small saucepan, heat the wine to just below the boiling point. Remove from heat and add the honey. Stir well to dissolve. Add the juice, parsley, and seasonings and mix well. Set aside.

Chickens, split *or* Cornish hens, whole, skin on, bone in	five 2½ lb. birds
Scallions, white and green parts, chopped	10
Salt and black pepper	as needed

Separate the skin from the breast meat and fill space with the chopped scallions. Place chicken halves cut side down in a glass or stainless-steel roasting pan. Pour the marinade over the chicken halves and turn to coat all sides. Salt and pepper to taste, cover and refrigerate overnight.

(Continued)

*Bitter orange juice, the juice of Seville oranges, is sold bottled. If not available, substitute a 50/50 mixture of fresh orange juice and lime or lemon juice.

Chicken stock	8 oz. or as needed

Add the stock to the pan and roast the chickens in a 350 degree F oven for 40–50 minutes, or until the chickens are done. Baste every 10 minutes with the combination of stock and marinade in the pan.

Serve with fried plantains and rice. Garnish with fresh orange slices.

CHICKEN SANCHOCHO
St. Martin

Yield: 10–12 servings

Marinade:

Onion, diced	8 oz.
Lime juice, fresh squeezed	4 oz.
Corn oil	2 oz.
Poultry seasoning	1 tbsp.
Cumin powder	1 tbsp.
Nutmeg, grated	1 tsp.
Salt and black pepper	to taste

Mix the onion, lime juice, oil, and seasonings thoroughly in a mixing bowl large enough to hold the vegetables listed below.

Tomatoes, peeled and chopped	1 lb.
Green bell peppers, seeded and diced	1 lb.
Celery, peeled and chopped	12 oz.
Scallions, white and green parts, chopped	8–10

Add these vegetables and blend thoroughly.

Chicken parts, bone in, skin on	8 lb.

Trim the chicken pieces of any excess fat and skin. Place the chicken in a single layer in a glass or stainless-steel pan. Cover all surfaces of the chicken with the marinade. Cover pan tightly and refrigerate overnight.

Chicken stock	as needed

Place the chicken and its marinade in a stew pot. Add enough chicken stock to cover and bring to a boil. Lower heat and simmer for 30–40 minutes, skimming as needed. When done, let cool, then remove the chicken from the bones. Discard skin and bones. Pull chicken into bite-sized pieces and reserve. Strain the broth and discard all of the vegetable solids. Degrease the broth and reserve.

Yams, white, peeled, small dice	2 lb.
Cabbage, white, shredded	2 lb.
Calabaza*, small dice	1 lb.
Corn, kernels only	6 cobs
Carrots, thick sliced	1 lb.
Plantains, green, peeled and sliced	4–5

Just prior to serving, bring the broth to a boil. Add the vegetables, lower heat, and simmer until the vegetables are barely tender. Add the chicken and heat through. Serve in large, deep, heated bowls. (Individual servings may also be prepared in the same manner.)

Other vegetables may be substituted or used in different quantities. No accompaniments are necessary; Chicken Sanchocho is a complete meal in itself.

CHICKEN FRICASSÉE
Puerto Rico

Yield: 10 servings

Marinade:

Vinegar, red wine	6 oz.
Achiote oil	4 tbsp.
Garlic, minced	2 tsp.
Oregano	2 tbsp.
Salt	1 tsp.
Black pepper	1 tsp.
Chicken breasts, boned and skinned	ten 8–10-oz. breasts

Mix together the vinegar, oil, garlic, and seasonings. Rub the mixture on all surfaces of the chicken breasts. Place the breasts in a glass or stainless-steel pan, cover, and refrigerate overnight.

(Continued)

*If not available, use butternut or Hubbard squash.

Sauce:

Vegetable oil	2 oz.
Onion, chopped	1 lb.
Smoked ham, diced	8 oz.
Tomatoes, peeled, seeded, and chopped	2 lb.
Chicken stock	12 oz.
Red pepper, hot, left whole	1 – 2
Bay leaf	2

In a heavy saucepan, heat the oil over moderate heat and sauté the onions until soft. Add the ham and continue to cook for another few minutes. Add the tomatoes, stock, red pepper, and bay leaf and bring to a boil. Lower heat to a simmer.

Salt and black pepper	to taste

Remove chicken from the marinade and return it to the refrigerator, covered, until needed. Add the marinade and any other juices in the pan to the sauce and simmer for 30 – 40 minutes. Add salt and pepper. Let sauce cool and reserve.

Vegetable oil	as needed
Potatoes, cooked, cut in 1-inch cubes	as needed

To prepare an individual serving: Heat oil in a small skillet. Sauté a marinated chicken breast on one side until it begins to brown slightly. Turn to brown the other side, then add enough sauce to cover. Cover skillet and place in a 400 degree F oven for 10 minutes. Remove from oven and add 3 – 4 tbsp. of cooked potato cubes. Return to oven for another 5 minutes, or until the chicken is cooked through.

Garnish with chopped, pitted green olives, capers, and a julienne of peeled and seeded sweet red bell peppers. Serve with white rice.

CHICKEN BREASTS STUFFED WITH COCONUT *Cuba*

Yield: 10 servings

Stuffing:

Butter, whole	5 oz.
Coconut, fresh, grated	12–15 tbsp., lightly packed
Cilantro leaves, fresh, chopped	10 sprigs

In a small sauté pan, heat the butter over low to medium heat until it begins to foam. Add the grated coconut and the chopped cilantro. Lower heat and cook for 5–6 minutes. Let cool and refrigerate until the butter begins to harden.

Chicken breasts, boned and skinned	ten 8-oz. breasts
Salt and white pepper	as needed

Remove the tenders. Place breasts and tenders between sheets of waxed paper and pound with a mallet or the side of a heavy cleaver until the breast meat is a uniform thickness, about ⅛-inch. Pound the edges of the larger pieces a bit thinner. Be careful not to tear the meat. Lightly salt and pepper each piece.

Spread the coconut mixture evenly over the larger pieces of chicken to about a ½ inch from the edges. Place the tenders in the center of the larger pieces over the coconut mixture. Fold the sides of the bottom piece of chicken over the tenders. Starting at the narrow end, roll up, then refrigerate, seam-side down, for at least 1 hour before using.

Butter, whole, melted	as needed
Chicken stock	as needed

Brush a baking pan just large enough to hold the chicken breasts with melted butter. Place the rolled breasts in the pan, seam-side down. Brush the chicken with melted butter, then add enough chicken stock to just cover. Bake in a 350 degree F oven, covered, for 25–30 minutes, or until the chicken is done.

Serve on a bed of rice with some of the pan juices to which some grated coconut has been added. Sprinkle some shredded coconut on top. For a single serving, use an individual-serving, heatproof dish. Accompany with any cooked, green, leafy vegetable.

CHICKEN IN COCONUT SAUCE   *Martinique*

Yield: 10–12 servings

Vegetable oil	2 oz.
Onion, small dice	1½ lb.
Garlic, minced	2 tsp.
Mushrooms, sliced thin	¾ lb.

Heat the oil in a heavy saucepan over moderate heat. Sauté the onion until soft. Add the garlic and mushrooms and cook until the mushrooms begin to brown lightly.

Coconut milk	1 qt.
Parsley	5 sprigs
Thyme, fresh	5 sprigs
Hot pepper, green, left whole	1 or to taste
Salt and white pepper	to taste

Add the coconut milk, herbs, and the hot pepper. Simmer for 30 minutes. Add salt and pepper. Strain and discard the herbs and the hot pepper.

Grated coconut	2 oz.

Add, mix well, and let cool. Reserve.

Oil, vegetable *or* coconut	as needed
Chicken breasts, boned and skinned	ten 8–10-oz. breasts

To prepare an individual serving: Heat the oil over medium heat and sauté the chicken breast until it is lightly browned. Add 3–4 oz. of the coconut sauce, cover, and simmer 10–12 minutes, or until the chicken is done. (Cooking time will vary according to the thickness of the breast.)

Variation: Substitute 2–3 tbsp. of curry powder and a ½ tsp. of saffron for the herbs and hot pepper. Serve over a bed of white rice.

CHICKEN WITH CILANTRO AND APPLE   *Cuba*

Yield: 10 servings

Butter	2 oz.
Oil	2 oz.
Onion, small dice	1½ lb.
Apples, tart	2 lb.
Granny Smith, peeled and chopped	2 lb.
Garlic, minced	2 tsp.
Cilantro leaves, chopped	7 – 8 sprigs
Ginger root, grated	1 tbsp.
Cumin powder	1 tsp.
Turmeric	½ tsp.
Salt and white pepper	to taste

In a heavy saucepan, heat the butter and oil over medium heat. Sauté the onions until just soft. Add the apples, garlic, cilantro, and seasonings. Mix well, cover, and cook, over low heat, until the apples are soft. Adjust seasonings. Let cool, then refrigerate until needed.

Chicken breast	6 – 8 oz.
Butter, clarified	1 tbsp.

To prepare an individual serving: Cut 6 – 8 oz. of the chicken breast into 1-inch pieces. In a small sauté pan, heat the clarified butter over medium to high heat. Sauté the chicken pieces on all sides until lightly browned. Add 4 – 5 oz. of the onion/apple mixture and heat through. Cover the pan and finish in a 400 degree F oven for 5 – 8 minutes or, simmer, covered, on top of the stove.

Serve with white rice and garnish with whole sprigs of fresh cilantro.

ALMOND CHICKEN   *Panama*

Yield: 10 servings

Almonds, blanched	10 oz.

Toast the almonds until they are light brown. Reserve 2 – 3 oz. for garnish and grind the others fine.

(Continued)

Olive oil	2 oz.
Chicken breasts, boned and skinned	ten 8-oz. breasts
Flour	as needed

Heat the oil in a heavy skillet. Lightly dust the chicken in flour and sauté on both sides until light brown. Place the chicken breasts in a shallow baking pan just large enough to hold them.

Grapes, red or white, seedless	1 lb.
Pineapple, fresh	10 oz.
Orange juice	8 oz.
White wine, dry	8 oz.
Sugar *or* honey	1½ oz.
Thyme	to taste
Cloves	to taste
Salt	to taste
White pepper, ground	to taste

Wash the grapes and remove all stems. Dice the pineapple. Mix these fruits with the remaining ingredients and pour the mixture over the chicken, distributing the fruit evenly over the chicken. Cover the pan and bake at 350 degrees F for 30 minutes. Uncover the pan and bake for another 10 minutes.

Garnish portions with a fine julienne of candied orange peel and the reserved toasted almonds.

CHICKEN WITH CORN AND ZUCCHINI   *Mexico*

Yield: 10 servings

Lard *or* oil	2 oz.
Chickens, split, bone in, skin on	five 2¼-lb. birds

Heat the lard or oil in a heavy skillet over medium to high heat. Brown the chicken on all sides and place in a single layer in a roasting pan.

Onion, chopped	1½ lb.
Garlic, minced	1 tbsp.
Cumin, ground	1–2 tsp.
Tomatoes, peeled and seeded	3 lb.
Jalapeños, seeds and ribs removed, minced	2
Salt and pepper	to taste

In the same skillet, sauté the onions until they begin to color. Add the garlic and cumin and cook for another minute. Add the tomatoes, jalapeños, and salt and pepper. Simmer until most of the liquid has evaporated. Adjust seasonings, then pour this mixture over the chicken. Cover and place in a 350 degree F oven for 30 minutes, or until the chicken is cooked through.

Zucchini, cut in ½ inch rounds	2 lb.
Corn, kernels cut from cob	10 ears

Add the zucchini and corn to the roasting pan about 10 minutes before the chicken is done. Serve chicken surrounded with the zucchini, corn, and tomato sauce.

A good buffet entrée. If using chicken breasts, adjust cooking time to 20 minutes.

BROILED CHICKEN BREASTS IN A TOMATILLO-ORANGE MARINADE   *Mexico*

Yield: 10 servings

Marinade:

Tomatillos	1½ lb.
Water	as needed

Remove the papery husks from the tomatillos and wash. Place in a small saucepan of boiling water, lower heat, and simmer for 3–4 minutes. Drain, then place the tomatillos into the bowl of a food processor fitted with a steel blade.

Anaheim chilies	2

Split the chilies lengthwise. Remove the seeds and ribs. Place the chilies under a broiler flame or in a very hot oven until the skins begin to char. Add to the tomatillos in the bowl of the food proceessor.

(Continued)

Onion, chopped	8 oz.
Orange juice	4 oz.
Lime juice	2 oz.
Garlic, chopped	2 tsp.
Oregano	1 tbsp.
Salt	2 tsp.
Cayenne pepper	1 tsp.
Black pepper	1 tsp.
Cumin, ground	1 tsp.
Sugar	to taste

Add the onion, juices, garlic, and seasonings to the food processor bowl and puree.

Chicken breasts, boned, skin on	ten 8–10-oz. breasts

Place the breasts in a single layer in a glass or stainless-steel pan. Pour the marinade over the chicken, turning to cover on all sides. Cover and refrigerate overnight.

To serve, broil chicken, turning frequently and basting often with some of the marinade.

Serve with rice. The marinade may also be used as a sauce for the rice. Bring the marinade to a boil, then simmer for 2–3 minutes.

GRILLED CHICKEN WITH SOFRITO   *Cuba*

Yield: variable

Sofrito (see the recipes in the "Regional Flavorings" section)	as needed
Chicken	variable

Breasts, broiler parts, or Cornish hens, split and butterflied, may be used. Rub the chicken with the sofrito mixture on all sides, place in a stainless-steel or glass container, cover tightly, and refrigerate overnight. When serving, grill the chicken over medium heat until cooked through, about 10 minutes per side.

CORNISH HENS WITH PINEAPPLE   *Caribbean*

Yield: 10 servings

Cornish hens *or* small broilers	5
Vegetable oil	1 oz.

Onion, diced	1½ lb.
Garlic, minced	2 tbsp.
Tomato, peeled and chopped	2 lb.
Pineapple, fresh, large dice	2 lb.
Sherry, dry	6 oz.
Vinegar	4 oz. or to taste
Cinnamon stick	2–3 inch
Clove, powdered	½ tsp.
Salt and white pepper	to taste

Split the hens in two and trim excess fat and skin. Heat the oil in a large skillet over medium to high heat and sauté until lightly browned. Place the hens skin-side up in a small roasting pan. Reserve.

Using the same skillet, sauté the onions over medium heat until soft. Add the garlic and cook for another minute. Add the tomato and pineapple with their juices, and the sherry, vinegar, and seasonings. Simmer for 30 minutes. Adjust the seasonings if necessary. Remove the cinnamon stick and discard.

Pour the tomato/pineapple mixture over the hens. Cover the roasting pan and place in a 350 degree F oven for 45 minutes, or until tender and cooked through. Remove the hens and keep in a warm place. Reduce sauce, if necessary.

Serve a halved hen on a bed of white rice. Spoon the sauce on top and sprinkle with chopped, fresh cilantro or curly parsley.

CHICKEN PIBIL   *Yucatan*

Yield: 10 servings

Marinade:

Achiote paste (see the recipe in the "Regional Flavorings" section)	2 tbsp.
Garlic, crushed	1 tbsp.
Orange juice, fresh squeezed	16 oz.
Wine vinegar *or* lime juice, fresh squeezed	4 oz.

Combine the achiote paste, garlic, juice, and vinegar thoroughly.

(Continued)

Chicken breasts, boned and skinned	ten 8–10-oz. breasts

Place the chicken breasts in a glass or stainless-steel pan and coat with the marinade. Cover and refrigerate overnight.

Aluminum foil *or* parchment paper	10 pieces
Butter *or* oil	as needed

Fold foil or paper in half. Cut each folded piece 2 inches larger, on all sides, than the chicken breast it will enclose. Brush softened butter or oil over foil or parchment paper, then place a single portion of chicken in the middle. Spoon a small amount of the marinade on top. Fold the edges to make a tight envelope. If using parchment paper, brush top lightly with melted butter. Refrigerate until needed. To serve: Place packet(s) as needed on a baking sheet and bake in a 400 degree F oven for 10–15 minutes, or until cooked through. (Cooking time will vary, depending on the thickness of breast meat.)

Serve the chicken directly in its packet. Cut foil in an attractive leaflike pattern prior to serving to make a more decorative presentation. This dish was originally prepared wrapped in banana leaves and baked in an earthen oven called a *pib*. Serve with rice and beans.

CHICKEN WITH OLIVES AND CORN   *Colombia*

Yield: 12 servings

Flour	as needed
Chickens, cut in 8 parts each: legs (2), thighs (2), and breasts split behind the wing joint (4)	three 3-lb birds
Oil and butter, 50/50	as needed

Dredge the chicken parts in flour. Shake to remove excess. In a heavy skillet, sauté the chicken until brown on all sides. When done, transfer the chicken parts to a roasting pan or casserole. Discard most of the fat in the skillet, leaving 2–3 tbsp. to sauté the vegetables.

Onion, chopped	1½ lb.	Using the same skillet, sauté the vegetables over low heat until soft.
Red bell pepper, seeded and chopped	12 oz.	
Carrot, diced	8 oz.	
Celery, diced	8 oz.	
Garlic, minced	2 tsp.	
Tomatoes, fresh, peeled, seeded, and chopped	2 lb.	Add the tomatoes and seasonings to the skillet. Deglaze the pan and simmer for 10–15 minutes. Adjust seasonings to taste. Pour over chicken parts, cover, and place in a 350 degree F oven for 30 minutes.
Cumin, ground	2 tsp.	
Salt and black pepper	to taste	
Green olives stuffed with pimentos, chopped	4 oz.	Add the olives and corn to the chicken. Cover and return to the oven for 10–15 minutes, or until the chicken is cooked through.
Corn, kernels cut from the cob	4–5 ears	

Serve with rice or potatoes.

CHICKEN IN CREAM AND TWO PEPPERS *Guatemala*

Yield: 10 servings

Butter, clarified	2 oz.	Heat the butter in a skillet and sauté the peppers, onions, and garlic until lightly browned. Sprinkle lightly with salt and pepper, stir, and reserve until needed.
Red bell peppers, seeded and sliced thin	1½ lb.	
Green bell peppers, seeded and sliced thin	1½ lb.	
Onion, sliced thin	1 lb.	
Garlic, chopped	1 tbsp.	
Salt and pepper	to taste	

Butter, clarified	as needed
Chicken breasts, boned and skinned	ten 8 – 10 oz. breasts
Flour	as needed
Heavy cream	3 – 4 oz. per serving

To prepare an individual serving: heat the clarified butter in a small skillet over medium heat. Dredge the chicken breast lightly in flour. Sauté on one side until lightly browned. Turn the chicken and add 5 – 6 oz. of the reserved peppers mixture and the heavy cream. Cover and finish in a 400 degree F oven for 10 – 12 minutes, or until the chicken is cooked through.

Variation: Reduce the quantity of peppers to 1 lb. each. Sauté the peppers, onion, and garlic, then add 1½ lb. of peeled, seeded, and chopped tomatoes and 5 – 6 tbsp. of chopped, fresh mint leaves. Simmer until most of the liquids have evaporated. Add salt and pepper and reserve until needed.

CHICKEN WITH BANANAS   *Brazil*

Yield: 10 servings

Lemon juice	8 oz.
Salt	1 tsp.
White pepper	1 tsp.
Jalapeño, seeds and ribs removed, then minced	1
Chicken breasts, boned and skinned	ten 8 – 10 oz. breasts

Combine the lemon juice, salt, pepper and jalapeño and set aside. Place the chicken in a glass or stainless-steel pan and pour the marinade on top. Cover and refrigerate for at least 4 hours, turning the chicken once or twice to coat well.

Olive oil	1 oz.
Onion, small dice	1 lb.
Tomatoes, peeled and chopped	3 lb.
Chicken stock	8 oz.
Sugar	1 tsp. or to taste
Salt and black pepper	to taste

In a small saucepan, heat the oil over medium heat and sauté the onion until soft. Add the tomatoes, stock, and seasonings and bring to a boil. Lower heat and simmer until the mixture begins to thicken. Remove from heat, let cool, and reserve.

Oil *or* clarified butter	as needed
White wine, dry	as needed

To prepare an individual serving: Heat the oil over medium to high heat in a small skillet. Sauté chicken breast until lightly browned on one side. Turn the chicken over and add 2–3 oz. of the tomato sauce and a splash of white wine. Cover and continue cooking in a 400 degree F oven for 8–10 minutes, depending on the thickness of the chicken breast. Remove skillet from oven and uncover.

Bananas	½ per serving
Parmesan cheese, grated	as needed
Butter, whole	as needed

Slice the banana in half lengthwise. Place on top of the chicken and sprinkle with grated cheese. Dot with butter, return to the oven, and cook for another 5 minutes, or until the chicken is done.

CHICKEN ACHIOTE   *Mexico*

Yield: 12 servings

Chickens, quartered	three 3-lb. birds
Salt and pepper	as needed

Wash, pat dry, and season the chicken.

Corn oil	2 oz.
Achiote seeds	2 tsp.

In a heavy skillet, heat the oil over medium heat and sauté the chicken pieces until browned. Reserve the chicken in a warm plate and strain the fats into a small saucepan. Add the achiote seeds and oil to the chicken fat and bring to a simmer. Cook, stirring, for 3–4 minutes, or until the oil turns a deep red. Strain the oil and discard the seeds. Return the achiote oil to the skillet.

(Continued)

Onion, chopped	12 oz.
Tomato, chopped	1½ lb.
Green pepper, chopped	8 oz.
Oregano, chopped	1 tsp.
Cilantro leaves, chopped	2 tbsp.
Chicken stock	8 oz.
Salt and pepper	to taste

In the same skillet, sauté the vegetables and herbs over medium heat until soft. Return the chicken to the pan. Add the chicken stock and salt and pepper. Simmer, partially covered, for 20–30 minutes, or until the chicken is done.

Serve with white rice and fried, very ripe, plantains.

CHICKEN IN GREEN ALMOND SAUCE   *Mexico*

Yield: 10 servings

Oil, olive *or* vegetable	2 oz.
Onion, chopped	1 lb.
Garlic, minced	1 tsp.

In a heavy skillet, heat the oil over medium heat and sauté the onions until soft. Do not brown. Add the garlic and continue to cook for another minute. When done, transfer to the bowl of a food processor.

Almonds, lightly toasted, and ground	8 oz.
Cilantro leaves	1 bunch
Parsley, flat leaf	1 bunch
Jalapeños, seeded, ribs removed, chopped	2

Add the almonds, herbs, and jalapeños to the onions and garlic, and, using a steel blade, pulse until you have a coarse puree.

Chicken stock	1 qt.
Salt and black pepper	to taste

In a heavy-bottomed saucepan, bring the chicken stock to a boil. Add the puree, mix well, and simmer, uncovered, for 20 minutes. Reduce volume by one-quarter. Add salt and pepper. Let cool and reserve.

Chicken breasts, boned and skinned	ten 5–7-oz. breasts	To prepare an individual serving: Sauté the chicken breast in a small amount of oil until it begins to color on one side. Turn the breast over and add 2–3 oz. of sauce. Cover and place in a 400 degree F oven for 8–10 minutes, or until the chicken is done. (Cooking time will vary, depending on the thickness of the meat.)
Oil	as needed	

Serve on a bed of white rice and with a side portion of black beans.

CHICKEN OR TURKEY WITH MOLE VERDE   *Mexico*

Yield: 10–12 servings

Pepitas, shelled, raw, pumpkin seeds	12 oz.	Use unsalted pepitas. Place them in a blender or processor and pulverize. Transfer to a stainless-steel mixing bowl and reserve.
Tomatillos	1 lb.	Remove the papery husks and wash the tomatillos. Place in rapidly boiling water for 1–2 minutes. Drain and place in the bowl of a food processor fitted with a steel blade.
Poblano chilies	1 lb.	Roast the chilies in a hot oven until the skins begin to char. Remove from oven, cover with a towel for 5 minutes, then peel. Slit in half and remove the seeds. Place in the food processor along with the tomatillos.
Onion, chopped	8 oz.	Place the onion, garlic, and cilantro into the bowl of the processor and puree.
Garlic, minced	1 tbsp.	
Cilantro leaves, chopped	10 sprigs	
Reserved pepitas		Add the pepitas and pulse a few times to mix thoroughly.
Oil, corn	2 oz.	Heat the oil in a sauce pan over medium heat. Add the contents of the processor, stir well and cook, stirring, for 2–3 minutes.

(Continued)

Chicken stock	24 oz.
Salt and pepper, white	to taste

Add the chicken stock in a slow steady stream and stir until the sauce reaches the boiling point. Lower heat and simmer for 15–20 minutes. Stir frequently and do not allow to boil. When done, add salt and pepper to taste then let cool and reserve.

Chicken breast or turkey fillets; (chicken parts, bone in, may also be used)	as needed

Poach poultry until just done. This may be done in advance and reserved. To prepare an individual serving, place 5–7 ounces of cooked poultry in 4–5 oz. of the sauce. Heat through over low to medium heat. Do not boil.

Serve with white rice and garnish with wedges of melon, fresh papaya or pineapple.

MEATS

VEAL STEW IN BAKED SQUASH   *Argentina*

Yield: 10–12 servings

Oil	2 oz.
Veal *or* beef, trimmed of all fat and cut into 1-inch cubes	3–3½ lb.

In a large skillet, heat oil over medium to high heat and sauté the meat until light brown. Remove from skillet and place in a stew pot.

Onion, diced	1 lb.
Green bell pepper, chopped	12 oz.
Jalapeños, deveined, seeded, and minced fine	2
Tomatoes, peeled, seeded, and cut into eighths	2 lb.

Using the same skillet, reduce the heat to low and sauté the onions and green bell peppers until soft. Add the jalapeños and tomatoes and simmer for another 3–4 minutes. Add this mixture to the stew pot.

Chicken stock	16 oz.
White wine, dry	16 oz.
Oregano	1 tbsp.
Sugar	2 tsp.
Salt and black pepper	to taste

Add the stock and wine and bring to a boil. Lower heat to simmer, add the seasonings, and cook until the meat is tender. (Cooking time will vary depending on type and cut of meat.) Adjust seasonings. Let cool and reserve.

Batatas (boniatos), cut in ½-inch cubes	1½ lb.
Potatoes, cut in ½-inch cubes	1½ lb.

Cook the batatas and potatoes in boiling water until just tender. Place in iced water when done. When cool, add to the meat and reserve.

Rice, long grain	6 oz.

Cook the rice until just tender, then add to the meat and vegetables.

(Continued)

Fruits (mixture of sliced peaches, pears, and apricots)	1½ lb.	Add the fruits and thoroughly blend all ingredients. Reserve.

Squash, winter (Hubbard or other hard-shelled variety)	10–12	Select squash that are firm and unblemished and are of an appropriate size to contain an individual serving. Cut off the stem end to make a lid and reserve. Trim the opposite end so that the squash will stand solidly when baked. Core the centers of the squash, removing all seeds and stringy parts. Bake squash in a 350 degree F oven until just tender. Do not overcook. When done and cool enough to handle, stuff each of the squash with the meat and fruit mixture. Place a squash lid on each and pin down with toothpicks. Reserve in refrigerator until needed. To serve, bring to room temperature, then place in a 400 degree F oven for 20–25 minutes, or until heated through. If reheating directly from the refrigerator, allow for additional cooking time.

For buffet service, large pumpkins or calabaza may be used. Follow the same procedure.

FRESH TONGUE IN PEPPER SAUCE   *Ecuador*

Yield: 10–12 servings

Oil	2 oz.	In a heavy skillet, heat the oil over low heat and sauté the vegetables until they begin to caramelize. Reserve.
Onion, diced	1 lb.	
Carrot, thick sliced	1 lb.	
Celery, thick sliced	8 oz.	

Beef tongue, fresh, *or* calf tongues, fresh	4–5 lb. *or* two 2½-lb. tongues	Trim the thick end of the tongue of all glandular tissue, fat, and bones. Place tongue in a small stockpot and add enough water to cover. Bring to a boil. Lower heat and simmer for 30 minutes. Skim liquid as necessary.

Cilantro	10 sprigs
Bay leaf	2
Salt and black peppercorns	to taste

Add the sautéed vegetables, herbs, and seasonings and continue to simmer for another 2½ hours, or until the tongue is tender. If using calf tongues, reduce total cooking time by 1 hour. Let tongue cool in the stock. When cool enough to handle, peel off the skin. Strain and degrease the stock and reserve.

To serve cold as a light luncheon or appetizer dish, thinly slice the tongue and garnish with a salsa and fresh garden vegetables. To serve hot, place sliced tongue in stock and heat through over very low heat. Accompany with the following sauce.

Pepper Sauce:

Oil, olive *or* vegetable	1 oz.
Red bell pepper, diced	1 lb.
Onion	8 oz.
Garlic, minced	2 tsp.
Dry mustard	2 tbsp. or to taste

In a small saucepan, heat the oil over low to medium heat and sauté the red pepper and onion until very soft. Add the garlic and continue to cook for another minute. Add the mustard and blend thoroughly.

Parsley, flat leaf, finely chopped	6 – 7 sprigs

Add 24 oz. of the reserved tongue stock and parsley and simmer, partially covered, for 30 minutes. Strain, reserving the liquids. Puree all of the vegetables in a food processor then return the puree to the stock.

Capers	1 tbsp.
Lemon juice, fresh squeezed	to taste
Salt and black pepper	to taste

Add the capers, lemon juice, salt, and pepper and mix well. Reserve and reheat as needed.

SPARERIBS WITH VEGETABLES   *Puerto Rico*

Yield: 10–12 servings

Spareribs, cut into 2–3 rib sections	10 lb.
Flour	as needed
Salt and pepper	as needed

Dredge ribs in flour, salt, and pepper: 4 oz. flour, 1 tbsp. salt, 2 tbsp. black pepper. Shake off excess flour.

Vegetable oil	as needed

Heat oil in a large heavy skillet. Sauté the ribs until well browned. Place in a baking pan in a single layer and keep in a warm place.

Onion, thin sliced	1 lb.

Using the same skillet, sauté the onion until soft. Add to the ribs.

Chicken stock	2–3 cups
Cilantro leaves, chopped	1 bunch
Salt and pepper	to taste

Add the stock and cilantro to the ribs and place, covered, in a 350 degree F oven for 45 minutes. Add salt and pepper.

Carrots, sliced	1½ lb.
Potatoes, sliced thin	3 lb.
Green beans	1½ lb.

Boil the vegetables separately until just tender. Add to the ribs and heat through just before serving.

A good buffet item. Serve with white rice and fried plantains.

BRAISED BEEF STUFFED WITH CHORIZO   *Cuba*

Yield: 10–12 servings

Beef, eye round	5–6 lb.
Chorizo (See recipe— "Meats")	as needed

Trim the meat of fat. Insert a long, thin knife in the center of one end to make a hole running half the length of the eye round. Turn the meat around and repeat this process from the other end. Twist the knife in the hole to make it large enough to insert chorizo links from end to end. Allow the chorizo to protrude an inch or so from either end.

Slab bacon, sliced thin, then diced	4 oz.
Egg, hard boiled, cut in eighths	1–2
Olives, pimiento stuffed	as needed
Ham, sliced thin, then diced	4 oz.
Raisins	as needed
Mozzarella, fresh, cut in small cubes	as needed
Prunes, pitted and soaked	as needed
Salt and black pepper, coarsely ground	as needed

Make two more channels in the meat on either side of the one containing the chorizo. Alternating ingredients, stuff with bits of bacon, egg, olives, ham, raisins, mozzarella, and prunes until the channels have been filled. Seal the ends with pieces of bacon or ham. Generously salt and pepper the entire roast.

Flour	as needed
Oil	2 oz.

Lightly dust the roast with flour and, using a heavy skillet over medium to high heat, sear the meat on all sides. When well-seared, place the meat in a small roasting pan and reserve in a warm place.

Onion, diced	1 lb.
Green bell pepper, small dice	8 oz.
Garlic, chopped	1 tbsp.

Using the same skillet, sauté the vegetables over medium heat until the vegetables are soft.

Paprika	1 tbsp.
Ginger root, minced	2 tsp.
Oregano, dried	2 tsp.
Cumin, ground	1 tsp.
Bay leaf	2

Add the seasonings, stir well, and cook for another 2 minutes.

(Continued)

Sherry, dry	1 pt.
Orange juice	4 oz.
Beef stock	as needed

Raise heat to high and add the sherry. Bring to a rapid boil and deglaze the pan. Pour entire contents of pan over the eye round. Add the orange juice and enough stock to cover the meat half way. Cover roasting pan and place in a 350 degree F oven for 1½ hours, or until the meat is tender. Add more stock, if needed, during the cooking process. An alternate method of cooking would be to place the meat in a small casserole and simmer on top of the stove, covered, until tender.

When done, remove the meat to a warm place, cover, and let stand for at least 15–20 minutes before slicing. Degrease the pan liquids and pass solids through a food mill. Add pureed vegetables to the pan liquids and adjust seasoning if necessary. When serving, place a pool of the sauce on a heated plate and top with slices of the meat.

Serve with rice and fried plantains.

RABBIT WITH WHITE WINE AND PEARL ONIONS   *Peru*

Yield: 12 servings

Marinade:

Vegetable oil	6 oz.	Combine the oil, vinegar, garlic, and seasonings using a wire whisk.
Vinegar, white wine	4 oz.	
Garlic, minced	1 tbsp.	
Oregano, dried	1 tbsp.	
Rosemary, dried	1 tbsp.	
Cumin, ground	1 tbsp.	
Salt	2 tsp.	
Black pepper, coarsely ground	2 tsp.	

Rabbits, quartered	three 3-lb. rabbits	Place the rabbits in a single layer in a glass or stainless-steel pan. Pour the marinade on top and turn the rabbit pieces to coat well. Cover and refrigerate overnight.
Slab bacon, diced	8 oz.	In a large, heavy skillet, sauté the bacon over low to medium heat until all of the fat is rendered. Remove the bacon bits and reserve. Remove the rabbit from the marinade. Dry the pieces with a towel, then sauté them in the bacon fat on all sides until lightly browned.
White wine	as needed	Transfer the sautéed rabbit to a small roasting pan along with the marinade. Add enough white wine to just cover. Distribute the onions around the rabbit. Cover and place in a 350 degree F oven for 1 hour or until the rabbit is tender. When done, remove the rabbit, degrease the pan liquids, and reduce the sauce over high heat.
Pearl onions, peeled, root ends trimmed	40	

Serve with boiled potatoes and garnish with black olives.

RABBIT IN PORT WINE CHOCOLATE SAUCE   *Peru*

Yield: 12 servings

Slab bacon, cubed	8 oz.	In a large, heavy skillet, sauté the bacon until all of the fat has been rendered. Reserve bacon bits.
Rabbits, quartered	three 3-lb. rabbits	Using the same skillet, sauté the rabbit until lightly browned on all sides. Remove, place in a clean stew pot, and reserve in a warm place.
Onions, diced	1 lb.	Discard excess bacon fat and, using the same pan, sauté the onions until soft. Add the carrot, celery, and garlic and continue to cook, over low heat, for another 4–5 minutes.
Carrot, diced	8 oz.	
Celery, peeled and chopped	8 oz.	
Garlic, minced	1 tbsp.	

(Continued)

Flour, all-purpose	2 oz.	Add the flour, stir well to incorporate thoroughly, and cook for another 2–3 minutes.

Port wine	8 oz.	Add the wine, deglaze the pan, and let cook over medium heat until the liquid has evaporated. Add the stock and bring to a boil.
Chicken stock	2 qt.	

Chocolate, unsweetened, chopped	3 oz.	Add the chocolate and seasonings, lower heat to a simmer, and cook for 30 minutes, stirring occasionally. Pour the sauce over the reserved rabbit, cover, and simmer for 1 hour, or until the rabbit is tender. Adjust seasonings if necessary.
Cardamom, ground	1 tsp.	
Cloves, ground	½ tsp.	
Cayenne pepper	to taste	
Salt and pepper	to taste	

Serve with white rice and garnish with chopped, fresh cilantro leaves.

STEWED RABBIT   *Panama*   Yield: 12 servings

Rabbit	three 3-lb. rabbits	Clean the rabbit and rub with lemon. Cut the rabbit into quarters or smaller pieces, if desired.

Garlic, minced	2 tbsp.	Mix the garlic, seasonings, and oil thoroughly and rub on all sides of the rabbit pieces. Place in a glass or stainless-steel pan. Cover and refrigerate overnight.
Oregano	1 tbsp.	
Salt	2 tsp.	
Pepper	1 tbsp.	
Oil	enough to bind these ingredients	

Vegetable oil	as needed	Heat the oil in a heavy skillet and brown the rabbit on all sides. Remove the rabbit and reserve in a warm place.

Onion, sliced thin	1½ lb.
Tomatoes, peeled, seeded, and chopped	2 lb.
Bay leaf	2
Cinnamon	2-inch stick

In the same pan, sauté the onion until soft. Add the tomatoes and bay leaf. Bring to a boil, then lower heat and simmer for 15 minutes. Return the rabbit to the pan, add the cinnamon stick, cover, and simmer 50–60 minutes, or until the rabbit is very tender. Remove the bay leaf.

Green beans cut in pieces	as needed
Carrots, sliced	as needed
Potatoes, large dice	as needed

The vegetables may be precooked and refrigerated. To serve, add a 5–6-oz. combination of these vegetables per serving and reheat with the rabbit and pan liquids.

Serve with white rice.

RABBIT WITH PEANUT SAUCE   *Peru*

Yield: 12 servings

Rabbits, quartered	three 3-lb. rabbits
Flour	as needed
Salt and black pepper	as needed
Butter	1 oz.
Vegetable oil	2 oz.

Dredge the rabbit pieces lightly in seasoned flour. Heat the butter and oil in a large, heavy skillet and sauté on all sides until lightly browned. When done, remove the rabbit pieces and place in a stew pot.

Paprika	3 tbsp.
Onions, diced	1½ lb.
Jalapeño, seeded and minced	1 or to taste
Garlic, minced	1 tsp.
White wine, dry	8 oz.
Cumin, ground	2 tsp.
Chicken stock	as needed

Using the same skillet, sauté the paprika and cumin, stirring, for 1 minute. Then add the onions, jalapeño, and garlic, and sauté until the onions are soft. Add the white wine, bring to a boil, and deglaze the pan. Pour this mixture over the sautéed rabbit. Add enough chicken stock to just cover the rabbit, bring to a boil, then lower heat and simmer for 30 minutes.

(Continued)

| Ground peanuts | 8 oz. |
| Salt and black pepper | as needed |

Add the peanuts and stir well. Continue to simmer for another 20–30 minutes or until the rabbit is tender. Add salt and pepper.

Serve with whole boiled potatoes.

RABBIT WITH ORANGE SAUCE   *Chile*

Yield: 12 servings

Oil, olive *or* vegetable	3 oz.
Flour	as needed
Rabbits, quartered	three 3-lb. rabbits

In a large skillet, heat oil over medium to high heat. Dredge the rabbit in flour, then sauté on all sides until the rabbit is lightly browned. When done, transfer the pieces to a stew pot.

Onions, diced	1½ lb.
Garlic, minced	1 tsp.
White wine, dry	8 oz.

Using the same skillet, sauté the onions until soft. Add the garlic and cook for another minute. Add the wine and bring to a boil. Deglaze the pan and pour over the rabbit.

| Orange juice | as needed |
| Salt and white pepper | to taste |

Add enough orange juice to just cover the rabbit pieces and salt and pepper. Bring to a boil, then lower heat, cover the pot, and simmer for 45 minutes to an hour, or until the rabbit is tender. When done, transfer the rabbit to a warm place.

| Eggs, beaten | 3 |
| Salt and white pepper | to taste |

Strain the pot liquids. Discard the solids. Beat the eggs in a separate bowl. Add small amounts of the pot liquid to the eggs while stirring briskly with a wire whisk to temper. Return the beaten egg mixture to the remaining pot liquids. Adjust for salt and pepper and reserve. To serve, reheat rabbit as needed in sauce over low heat. When reheating the sauce, do not allow to boil.

Serve with noodles or white rice and garnish with chopped, hard boiled eggs, fresh orange slices, and chopped, fresh parsley.

RABBIT IN COCONUT MILK   *Colombia*

Yield: 12 servings

Marinade:

Cider vinegar	8 oz.
Garlic, minced	2 tbsp.
Salt	2 tbsp.
Black pepper, coarsely ground	2 tbsp.
Cumin, ground	1 tbsp.
Pepper, cayenne	1 tsp.

Combine the vinegar, garlic, and seasonings.

Rabbits, quartered	three 3-lb. rabbits

Place the rabbit pieces in a glass or stainless-steel pan and pour the marinade on top; to coat evenly. Cover and let marinate in the refrigerator overnight. When ready to cook, transfer the rabbit and the marinade to a large stew pot.

Achiote oil (see the recipe in the "Regional Flavorings" section)	3 tbsp.
Onion, diced	2 lb.
Tomatoes, peeled, seeded, and chopped	3 lb.
Chicken stock	as needed

In a heavy skillet, heat the achiote oil over low to medium heat and sauté the onions until soft. Add the tomatoes and simmer until the mixture begins to thicken. Pour this over the rabbit. Add enough chicken stock to barely cover. Bring liquids to a boil, lower heat, partially cover the pot, and simmer for 45 minutes to 1 hour, or until the rabbit is tender.

Coconut milk, thick	12 oz.

When done, remove the rabbit and keep warm. Reduce the cooking liquid by half over high heat. Remove from heat, and, stirring briskly, add the coconut milk. Return to low heat and heat through but do not boil.

Serve on a bed of white rice with the coconut sauce spooned on top.

PORK CHOPS WITH ORANGE SAUCE   *Mexico*

Yield: 1 serving

Slab bacon, diced	1 thick slice

In a small, heavy skillet, sauté the bacon until the fat is rendered. Remove bacon bits and reserve.

Dry mustard	½ tsp.
Pork chops, center cut	two 4-oz. *or* one 8-oz chop
Salt and black pepper	as needed

Rub the mustard over the surface of the chop(s). Sprinkle with a little salt and pepper, then sauté in the bacon fat until both sides are browned.

Onion, sliced thin	2 tbsp. approx.
Green bell pepper, sliced thin	2 tbsp. approx.
Garlic, minced	½ tsp.

Add the vegetables and cook for another minute.

Orange juice	2 oz.
Lemon *or* lime juice	1 oz.
White wine, dry	1 oz.

Add juices and wine, cover pan, and cook over low heat until the chops are tender. Adjust seasonings when done. Pour the pan liquids over the chops and garnish with the bacon bits.

Serve with white rice.

PORK IN ADOBO   *Mexico*

Yield: 12 servings

Pork shoulder, trimmed	5 lb.
Veal stock *or* water	1 qt.
Onion, whole	8 oz.
Celery	2 ribs
Salt	2 tsp.
Peppercorns	1 tsp.
Bay leaf	1

Cut the pork into 1½-inch cubes and place in a small saucepan with stock or water. Bring to a boil, then lower heat and simmer for 10 minutes, skimming as needed. Add onion, celery, and seasonings and continue to simmer until the pork is tender. Do not overcook. Remove pork and strain the cooking liquid; reserve separately. Discard the vegetables.

Lard *or* oil	4 oz.
Adobo paste	3 – 4 oz.

Heat the lard in a heavy skillet over medium heat, then brown the pork on all sides. When done, transfer the pork to a clean stew pot. Add the adobo paste to the skillet, lower heat, and cook, stirring, for 5 minutes.

Sugar	4 tbsp.
Cinnamon	1 – 2 tsp.
Cumin, ground	1 tsp.
Salt and black pepper	to taste

Add the seasonings to the adobo paste, stir well, and cook for 3 – 4 minutes. Add 1½ pt. of the reserved cooking liquid and bring to a boil. Deglaze the pan, then pour over the pork. Simmer until the sauce thickens. Adjust salt and pepper.

BEEF POT ROAST WITH CAPERS   *Venezuela*

Yield: 10 – 12 servings

Beef, bottom round	5-lb. piece
Pork fat, cut in strips ¼-inch square by 2 inches longer than the piece of meat	10 – 12 strips
Capers	as needed

Lard the beef with the pork strips. (Chill the strips to make handling easier.) Push a channeled larding needle through the meat. Then place a strip of the pork fat into the channel and pull the strip through the meat. Repeat this process to create an attractive checkered pattern when sliced. Trim the ends of the pork fat and, using a blunt skewer, push capers into the beef around the pork strips.

Onion, grated	8 oz.
Garlic, minced	1 tsp.
Salt	2 tsp.
Black pepper, coarsely ground	1 tsp.
Vinegar, red	as needed

Mix the vegetables and seasonings together, using a small amount of vinegar to create a smooth paste. Press this mixture firmly onto all surfaces of the meat. Place the meat in a stainless-steel or glass container, cover loosely with foil, and refrigerate overnight.

Vegetable oil	2 oz.
Brown sugar	as needed

Heat the oil in a heavy stew pot over medium-high heat. Sprinkle the meat with a light coating of brown sugar and brown on all sides.

(Continued)

Beef stock	1½ pint
Salt and black pepper	to taste

Add the beef stock, cover pot with a tightly fitting lid, and bring to a boil. Lower heat and simmer for approximately two hours, or until the meat is very tender. When done, remove meat, wrap in foil, and let rest in a warm place for 15–20 minutes before slicing. Degrease the pot liquids and adjust for salt and pepper. Serve with pot liquids spooned over slices of meat.

Serve with boiled yams, batata, or potato.

ROASTED PORK TENDERLOIN *Jamaica*

Yield: 10–12 servings

Scallions, white and green parts, chopped	10
Thyme	1 tbsp.
Sugar	1 tbsp.
Allspice, ground	2 tsp.
Nutmeg, ground	1 tsp.
Salt	1 tsp.
Black pepper	1 tsp.
Cinnamon, ground	½ tsp.
Corn oil	as needed

Combine all ingredients except the pork with enough oil to bind into a paste.

Pork tenderloin	4–5 lb.

Cover all surfaces of the pork with the flavoring mixture. Place in a glass or stainless-steel pan, cover tightly, and refrigerate overnight. Place on a rack in a 350 degree F oven for 45 minutes, or until the internal temperature reaches 160 degrees F.

To serve, arrange the slices in an attractive pattern and accompany with kidney beans and rice.

PICADILLO—THREE VERSIONS *Mexico*

Yield: 10–12 servings

Version 1:

Oil	1 oz.
Beef, ground twice	3½ lb.
Onion, diced	1½ lb.
Garlic, minced	1 tbsp.
Tomatoes, peeled, seeded, and chopped	2 lb.
Granny Smith *or* other tart apple, peeled, core removed, and chopped	4
Raisins	4 oz.
Olives, green, pimiento-stuffed, coarsely chopped	4 oz.
Jalapeños, seeded and minced	2 or to taste
Tomato puree	2 oz.
Oregano	to taste
Thyme	to taste
Salt and black pepper	to taste

In a large skillet, sauté the meat in the oil until browned. Remove from pan and place in a colander to drain excess fat.

Using the same pan, discard all but 2–3 tbsp. of fat and sauté onions until soft. Add the garlic and cook for another minute. Return meat to pan.

Add the remaining ingredients, mix well, and cook over low heat for 30 minutes, stirring occasionally.

Version 2:

Pork shoulder, trimmed of excess fat and cut into large cubes	4 lb.
Salt	to taste

Place pork in a small soup pot with enough water to cover. Bring to a boil, skim, then lower heat and simmer until tender. Remove meat and let cool. When cool enough to handle, shred meat and reserve.

(Continued)

Lard *or* vegetable oil	2 oz.
Onion, minced	1 lb.
Garlic, minced	2 tsp.
Tomato puree	2 oz.

In a large skillet, heat the lard over medium heat. Add the onions and garlic and sauté for 1–2 minutes, then add the tomato puree and continue to cook for another minute.

Tomatoes, peeled, seeded, and chopped fine	2 lb.
Raisins	4 oz.
Parsley, flat leaf, chopped	5–6 tbsp.
Chicken stock	1 pt.
Vinegar, red wine	1 oz. or to taste
Cinnamon stick	2 in.
Clove, ground	1 tsp.
Sugar	to taste
Salt and black pepper	to taste

Add the remaining ingredients to the pan and cook over medium-high heat until most of the liquid has evaporated. Add the pork, lower heat, mix well, and cook for another 20 minutes.

Version 3:

Lard *or* vegetable oil	2 oz.
Onion, chopped	1 lb.
Green bell pepper, chopped	1 lb.

In a large skillet, heat the oil over medium heat and sauté the onions and peppers until soft.

Beef, ground	3½ lb.
Plum tomatoes, canned, chopped coarsely	2 lb.
Raisins	4 oz.
Capers	2 tbsp.
Salt and black pepper	to taste

Add the remaining ingredients and mix well. Sauté until the meat has browned and most of the liquid has evaporated.

Picadillo has many other versions. Other optional ingredients include the addition of potatoes, peas, and mixed tropical fruits. Used as an entrée, it may be served in the center of a warm plate and surrounded with white rice and beans. Garnishes include guacamole, fried bananas, chopped egg whites, and toasted almonds. Picadillo is also popular as a filling for tamales, tacos, empanadas, and Anaheim or Poblano chilies.

PICADINHO   *Brazil*

Yield: 10–12 servings

Oil, olive *or* vegetable	2 oz.
Onion, chopped	1 lb.
Celery, chopped	4 oz.
Green bell pepper, seeded and chopped	4 oz.

In a large skillet, heat the oil over medium heat and sauté the onions until soft. Add the celery, green pepper, and garlic. Stir well and cook for 2 minutes more.

Top round, ground coarsely	3½ lb.
Tomatoes, peeled and chopped	2 lb.

Add the meat and brown well. Add the tomatoes and stir well to mix thoroughly. Cook over low heat for 15 minutes.

Beef stock *or* red wine, dry	1 pt.
Salt and black pepper	to taste
Hot red pepper flakes	to taste

Add the beef stock, salt, and peppers. Stir well. Cover partially and simmer for 1 hour, or until all of the liquid has been absorbed or evaporated.

Optional ingredients include pitted green olives, raisins, okra, chayote, and peas. Serve with Farofa (see the recipe in the "Beans, Rice, and Other Starches" section), rice, or mashed potatoes.

MATAMBRE (WITH TWO DIFFERENT STUFFINGS) *Argentina*

Yield: 10–12 servings

Flank steaks	two 2½-lb. steaks
Onion, sliced	8 oz.
Garlic, minced	1 tbsp.
Vinegar, red wine	6 oz.
Thyme, dried	1 tbsp.
Black pepper, coarsely ground	1 tsp.

Trim any excess fat and remove all membrane from each side of the steaks. Butterfly each steak, then cover each with plastic wrap or wax paper. Using a meat mallet or the side of a heavy cleaver, pound the meat to a uniform thickness. Place one of the steaks in a stainless-steel or glass tray. Mix the onion, garlic, vinegar, and seasonings together in a small bowl and distribute the mixture evenly over the surface of the meat. Place the second steak on top, press down firmly, and cover. Refrigerate overnight. When ready to cook, reserve the marinade, then overlap ends of steaks by 2 inches, with the grain of the meat aligned. (This will create a strip of meat double the length of a single steak.) Pound the overlapping edge with a mallet or the side of a heavy cleaver to join the two pieces of meat, then stuff, roll, and tie. An alternate method: Divide the stuffing in half and cook each steak separately.

Stuffing — Variation 1:

Spinach leaves, stem ends removed	1 lb.
Carrot sticks, blanched	as needed
Eggs, hard cooked, cut in quarters	5
Onion, sliced in thin rings	as needed
Parsley leaves, flat leaf, chopped	as needed
Chili pepper, dried, seeded, and crushed	to taste
Salt and black pepper	to taste
Beef stock	as needed

Wash spinach thoroughly and spread the leaves in an even layer over the meat. Make parallel rows of carrot sticks (across the grain), leaving just enough room between the rows to place the egg quarters. Place an even layer of onion slices on top, then sprinkle with parsley, chili pepper, salt, and pepper. Roll and tie with butcher's twine. Place in a casserole or small roasting pan with the marinade and enough stock to cover. Cook, covered, in a 375 degree F oven for 1 hour. Reserve cooking liquid as a base for soup.

Stuffing — Variation 2:

Veal, ground	12 oz.
Pork, ground	12 oz.
Spinach leaves, stem ends removed, leaves chopped	1 lb.
Egg, beaten	1 large
Garlic, minced	2 tsp.
Rosemary leaves, fresh chopped	2 tsp.
Clove, ground	½ tsp.
Nutmeg, ground	½ tsp.
Pistachios, peeled	2 – 3 oz.
Sherry, dry	2 – 3 oz.
Salt and black pepper	to taste
Beef stock	as needed

In a mixing bowl combine thoroughly all ingredients except the stock. Spread an even layer over surface of meat. Roll and tie. Place in a casserole and cover with stock. Bring to a boil, skim as needed, then lower heat to a simmer and cook, covered, for 1 hour. Let meat cool in liquid, then remove and place under a weighted tray until cold. Slice and serve at room temperature. Reserve cooking liquid as a base for soup.

May be served hot or cold as an entrée or appetizer. If served cold, let meat cool in cooking liquids. Then remove and press under weights in the refrigerator. This makes the Matambre firmer and, therefore, easier to slice. This method can also be used if the meat is cooked in advance, then sliced to reheat.

CALF'S LIVER SMOTHERED IN ONIONS   *Peru*

Yield: 1 serving

Achiote oil (see the recipe in the "Regional Flavorings" section)	1 tsp.
Slab bacon, small dice	2 tbsp.

In a small sauté pan, heat the oil over medium heat, then sauté the bacon until the fat has been rendered. Remove the bacon bits and reserve. Do not discard the fat.

(Continued)

Seasoned Flour:

Flour	as needed
Cumin, ground	as needed
Salt	as needed
White pepper, ground	as needed

Mix these ingredients: For every 4 oz. of flour, add 1 tbsp. ground cumin, 1 tbsp. salt, and 1 tsp. ground white pepper. Blend thoroughly.

Calf's liver	4–5 oz. per serving

Trim outer skin and remove any veins. Cut liver ½ to ¾ of an inch thick. Dredge in seasoned flour, taking care to cover all surfaces. Sauté immediately in the hot achiote oil and bacon drippings 2–3 minutes on each side, depending on the thickness of the slice. Do not overcook. The liver should be slightly pink on the inside when done. Remove from pan and reserve in a warm place.

Onions, red, thin sliced	4–6 oz.
Jalapeño, seeded and minced	½ tsp. or to taste
Garlic, minced	½ tsp.
Thyme leaves, fresh	½ tsp.
Salt and black pepper	to taste

Using the same skillet, sauté the onions over high heat, stirring frequently, for 1–2 minutes. Add the remaining ingredients and cook for another minute. When done, remove the onion mixture with a slotted spoon to eliminate as much fat as possible. Place the onions around the liver and garnish with the reserved bacon bits.

The last step may be done in advance and quickly reheated if faster service is necessary. Serve with boiled potatoes or white rice.

STUFFED FLANK STEAK   *Cuba*

Yield: 10–12 servings

Butter, whole	as needed
Onion, small dice	12 oz.
Carrots, grated	8 oz.
Brown sugar	3 tbsp.
Garlic, minced	1 tbsp.

In a skillet, heat butter over low heat until foamy. Add the onion and carrot and sauté until soft. Add the brown sugar and garlic and continue to cook for another 2 minutes. Remove from heat and let cool.

Olive oil	2 oz.
Lemon juice	3 oz.
Salt	1 tsp.
Black pepper, coarsely ground	1 tsp.

Add the oil, lemon juice, and seasonings, mix well, and reserve.

Flank steak, trimmed	two, 2½ lb. each
Smoked ham	as needed

Butterfly the steaks, then cover with butcher's paper. Using a meat mallet or the side of a heavy cleaver, pound the steaks to a uniform thickness. Divide the reserved vegetable and seasoning mixture into two equal parts. Spread this mixture evenly over one side of each steak. Top this with a single layer of smoked ham. Roll the steaks against the grain, and tie the meat securely.

Oil, olive *or* other vegetable	as needed
Flour	as needed
Red wine	4 oz.
Tomato, peeled, seeded, and chopped	2–3 lb.
Bay leaf	2
Salt and pepper	as needed

Heat oil in a casserole just large enough to hold the rolled flank steaks. Dust the meat lightly with flour and brown on all sides. Add the wine, tomato, and bay leaf. Cover the pot and simmer for 1½–2 hours, or until the meat is tender. Let meat rest for 20–30 minutes in a warm place before slicing. Adjust pan juices with salt and pepper, if needed. Serve meat with the pan juices.

FLANK STEAK IN WINE, LEMON, AND ORANGE MARINADE   *Cuba*

Yield: 10–12 servings

Marinade:

Port wine *or* Marsala	1 pt.
Honey	4 oz.
Ginger root, grated	2 oz.
Garlic, minced	2 tbsp.
Salt and black pepper	to taste
Orange juice, fresh squeezed	8 oz.
Lemon juice, fresh squeezed	4 oz.

Heat the wine to just below the boiling point. Remove from the heat and add the honey, ginger root, garlic, and seasonings. Cover and let steep for 15 minutes. Add the orange and lemon juice and mix well. Let cool completely before using.

Flank steak, trimmed of fat and membrane	5–6 lb. (two, 2½ lb. each)

Place the flank steak in a glass or stainless-steel pan. Pour the marinade on top. Cover and refrigerate overnight.

Broil or grill the steak over very hot coals or under high heat in the broiler for 3–5 minutes per side, depending on the thickness of the steak(s).

Grilled flank steak is best served rare with thin slices cut on a sharp angle diagonally across the grain. Accompany with black beans and rice.

STEAK WITH BUTTER AND LEMON SAUCE   *Cuba*

Yield: 1 serving

Sirloin steak, cut ¾-inch thick	8–10 oz.

Lightly pound steak between two sheets of waxed paper to a thickness of ½ inch.

Butter, clarified	as needed

Heat butter over high heat and sauté the steak quickly on both sides. Remove the steak to a warm plate.

Butter, whole	2 oz.
Lemon juice, fresh squeezed	3 oz.
Salt and black pepper, coarsely ground	as needed
Parsley, fresh, chopped	as needed

Discard clarified butter. Using the same skillet over medium heat, add the whole butter, lemon juice, and salt and pepper to taste. Stir with a wire whisk until thoroughly mixed and hot. Pour sauce over steak and garnish with fresh, chopped parsley.

Serve with fried potatoes and salad.

ROPA VIEJA ("OLD CLOTHES")   *Cuba*

Yield: 10–12 servings

Oil	as needed
Onion, large dice	1½ lb.
Carrot, peeled, 1-inch pieces	½ lb.
Celery, 1-inch pieces	½ lb.

Heat oil in a heavy skillet. Sauté the vegetables until they begin to brown. Reserve.

Flank steak *or* brisket of beef, trimmed of fat	5 lb.

Place the meat in a small soup pot with enough water to cover. Bring to a boil, then lower heat and simmer for 30 minutes, skimming as necessary. When liquid is clear, add the sautéed vegetables and continue to cook at a simmer for 1½ hours more, or until the meat is very tender. When done, let meat cool in the broth. Remove meat and strain the broth. Discard the vegetables and degrease the liquid. Reserve. Slice the meat across the grain into 2-inch strips. Then, using your fingers, shred the meat into strings. Reserve.

(Continued)

Oil, achiote (see the recipe in the "Regional Flavorings" section) *or* other vegetable oil	2 oz.
Onion, small dice	1½ lb.
Green bell pepper, seeded and chopped	1 lb.
Garlic, minced	1 tbsp.

Heat oil in a large, heavy skillet. Sauté the onions and peppers until soft. Add the garlic and continue to cook for another minute.

Tomato paste	4 tbsp.
Tomatoes, peeled and chopped	2 lb.
Chilies, mild green, seeds and ribs removed, chopped fine	6
Cayenne pepper	to taste
Salt	to taste

Add the tomato paste and cook for 1–2 minutes over medium heat. Add the remaining ingredients, along with 1 qt. of reserved stock. Bring to a boil, then lower heat and simmer for 30 minutes. Add cayenne and salt. Reserve.

To serve, combine the shredded beef and the sauce. Mix well. For individual servings, reheat as needed.

Serve with white rice and accompany with a mixed green salad.

PORK RIBS WITH PAPAYA SAUCE   *Cuba*

Yield: 10 servings

Marinade:

Papaya, fresh	1 lb.
White wine, dry	8 oz.
Water	8 oz.
Honey	6 oz.
Tomato paste	4 oz.
Vingar, red wine	2 oz.
Garlic, minced	1 tbsp.
Salt	1 tsp.
Black pepper	1 tsp.
Tabasco sauce	½ tsp.

Place the marinade ingredients in the bowl of a food processor and puree until smooth.

Baby back pork ribs	15 lb.

Cut the ribs into 1½ lb. sections, cracking the bone at the base of the ribs. Place the ribs in a glass or stainless-steel pan and add the marinade. Cover and refrigerate overnight.

Shake off excess marinade and place the ribs on a rack in an uncovered roasting pan. Roast ribs for ½ hour at 375 degrees F. Lower heat to 325 degrees F and continue to roast for another hour, basting with the marinade every 20 minutes.

RABBIT STEWED IN WHITE WINE   *Panama*

Yield: 12 servings

Vegetable oil	4 oz.
Garlic, sliced	2 tbsp.

In a large, heavy skillet, heat the oil over low heat and sauté the garlic until golden. Mash with a fork to extract the flavor, remove from oil, and discard.

Flour	as needed
Rabbit, cut into serving-sized pieces	three 3-lb. rabbits

Lightly flour the rabbit pieces and sauté over medium to high heat until browned. Remove from pan and reserve.

Onion, small dice	2 lb.
Poblano chilies, roasted, peeled, deseeded, and cut julienne	5–6
Tomatoes, plum, peeled and chopped	4 lb.
White wine	16 oz.
Thyme sprigs	2–3
Salt and black pepper	to taste

Using the same pan, lower heat and sauté the onions until soft. Add the rest of the ingredients and bring to a boil. Lower heat and simmer for 30 minutes. Add salt and pepper.

Return rabbit to pan and simmer for 45 minutes to 1 hour, or until the rabbit is tender. When done, remove the chilies, adjust seasonings, and serve the rabbit with the pan juices.

WHITE BEANS AND HAM   *Cuba*

Yield: 10–12 servings

White beans, great northern, cannellini, or lima	2 lb.

Wash beans and remove any debris. Soak beans in water overnight. Rinse well and discard the water. Transfer the beans to a stew pot.

Oil *or* lard	4 oz.
Onion, diced	1 lb.
Chicken stock	8 oz.
Sugar, dark brown	8 oz.
Vinegar, cider	4 oz.
Dry mustard	3 tsp.
Ginger, ground	3 tsp.
Salt and black pepper	to taste

In a separate saucepan, heat the fat and sauté the onions until soft. Add the chicken stock and bring to a boil. Add the sugar, vinegar, mustard, and seasonings and mix well. Taste for balance of flavors and adjust seasonings, if necessary. Add this mixture to the beans and combine thoroughly.

Ham hocks	4 large
Chicken stock	as needed

Place the ham hocks in the center of the stew pot surrounded on all sides, top, and bottom with the beans. Add enough chicken stock to just cover the beans.

Place a tight-fitting lid on the pot and bake in a 250 degree F oven for 5–6 hours. Do not stir. You may need to add small amounts of stock from time to time if the beans appear to be dry on top. Less cooking time may be required, depending on the type of bean used. When done and cool enough to handle, remove meat from ham hocks. Cut into small dice and return the meat to the beans. Mix well. Let cool and reserve.

Bean dishes keep well under refrigeration. Individual portions may be reheated as needed. Serve with white rice and salad.

ROAST PORK WITH PAPAYA   *Cuba*

Yield: 10–12 servings

Pork loin, boned	5 lb.
Uncured bacon, cut in small cubes	1 lb.

Trim excess fat and tie with butcher's twine to ensure uniform slices. In a heavy skillet, sauté the bacon until the fat is rendered. Remove the bacon bits and reserve. Brown the pork loin on all sides and transfer it to a casserole just large enough to hold the meat.

Onion, chopped	1 lb.
Garlic, minced	1 tsp.
Tomatoes, peeled and chopped	2 lb.

Discard all but several tablespoons of the rendered pork fat and sauté the onion until soft. Add the garlic and continue to cook for another minute. Add the tomato and bring to a boil. Deglaze the pan and pour over the pork loin.

Papaya juice	8 oz.
Chicken stock	as needed

Add the papaya juice to the casserole with enough chicken stock to bring the level of the liquids ½ to ¾ up the sides of the pork loin. Cover and simmer for 1–1½ hours, or until the pork is tender. Maintain this level of liquid during the cooking process by adding additional chicken stock if needed. When done, remove the pork to a warm place. Strain the pot liquids and degrease. Puree the vegetables and combine with the degreased pot liquids.

Papaya, fresh, ripe and sliced	as needed
Watercress sprigs	as needed

To serve, place a pool of the sauce on a warm plate and arrange 2 to 3 slices of the pork, depending on their thickness. Place slices of papaya on top of the pork, then sprinkle with the crushed bacon bits. Garnish with a large sprig of watercress or other green vegetable.

Serve with yellow rice, beans, and fried plantains.

PORK CHOPS ADOBO   *Mexico*   Yield: 10 servings

Pork chops	10 double, 8 – 10 oz. each
Adobo paste (See recipe)	as needed

Trim chops of excess fat, leaving a small rim of fat on the edge. Lightly score the fat. Rub each side of the chops with a liberal amount of adobo paste. In a glass tray, place the chops in a single layer and cover with foil. Refrigerate for 1 or 2 days before using.

Avocado, thin sliced	as needed
Onion rings, red, marinated in wine vinegar	as needed

Grill over coals or broil until done as desired. Garnish with thin slices of avocado, red onion rings, and salsa verde (see recipe) or tomatillo jalapeño salsa.

FRESH PORK STEWED WITH FRUITS   *Mexico*   Yield: 10 – 12 servings

Pork butt or shoulder	5 lb.

Trim fat, then cut pork into 1½-inch cubes. In a heavy skillet, render a bit of the pork fat, then sauté the cubes over high heat until they begin to brown lightly. Remove meat, place in a stew pot, and reserve.

Onion, small dice	2 lb.
Garlic, minced	1 tbsp.
Tomatoes, peeled and chopped	2 lb.
Lentils	1 lb.
Raisins	4 oz.
Chicken stock	as needed
Salt and black pepper	to taste

In the same skillet, sauté onion over medium heat until soft. Do not allow to brown. Add the garlic and cook for another minute. Add the tomatoes, lentils, and raisins and bring to a boil. Deglaze the pan and transfer contents to the stew pot containing the pork. Add enough stock to cover. Mix well and bring to a boil. Lower heat and simmer for 45 minutes to 1 hour, or until the pork is tender. Adjust salt and pepper. Reserve.

Vegetable oil *or* lard	as needed
Plantains, sliced in rounds	2 ripe
Pineapple, fresh, cut in 1-inch cubes	1 lb.

Just prior to serving, heat oil in a heavy skillet and sauté the fruits. Add to the reserved stew and heat through. To prepare an individual serving: Heat only the amount of pork stew needed. Sauté an appropriate amount of the fruits, add to the pork, then heat through.

Serve with a dish of sour cream on the side.

ROAST PORK LOIN
French Carribean

Yield: 10–12 servings

Flavoring Mixture:

Onion, grated	8 oz.
Ginger root, grated	2 oz.
Garlic, minced	1 tbsp.
Vegetable oil	1 oz.
Pickapeppa* sauce	2 tbsp.
Lemon juice	2 oz.
Hot pepper sauce	1 tsp.
Thyme	1 tsp.
Salt and black pepper, coarsely ground	to taste

Mix onion, ginger, garlic, oil, and seasonings thoroughly.

Sugar, brown	2 oz.
Water, warm	4 oz.

Dissolve the sugar in the warm water. Add to the above mixture and blend well.

(Continued)

---

*Available commercially.

Pork loin, boned and tied	5 lb.

Remove excess fat, leaving a small layer. In a heavy skillet, sear meat on all sides until well browned. Cover all surfaces of the meat with flavoring mixture. Place the loin on a double-thick sheet of aluminum foil large enough to completely enclose it and seal tightly. Wrap the loin, place in a small baking pan, and roast in 325 degree F oven for 1 hour.

Rum, dark	4 oz.
Lime juice, fresh squeezed	2 oz.
Sugar	1–2 tbsp. or to taste
Stock	as needed

When done, open foil, remove the pork to a warm place, and pour pan juices into a small heavy saucepan. Degrease, then add the rum, lime juice, and sugar to the pan juices. Add enough stock to bring liquids up to 16 oz. Bring to a boil, then lower heat and simmer for a few minutes. Adjust seasonings if necessary. Keep sauce warm. Spoon over slices of the pork when serving.

OXTAIL STEW   *Cuba*

Yield: 10–12 servings

Vegetable oil *or* lard	3 oz.
Oxtail, cut in 2-inch pieces	10 lb.
Flour	as needed

In a heavy skillet, heat the oil over medium to high heat. Dredge the oxtail pieces in flour and sauté until brown on all sides. When done, transfer to a heavy stew pot and reserve.

Onion, small dice	2 lb.
Green bell pepper, seeded and chopped	2 lb.
Garlic, minced	1 tbsp.

In the same skillet, sauté the onions and peppers over medium heat until soft. Add the garlic and continue to cook for another minute.

Red wine, dry	12 oz.
Beef stock	12 oz.
Tomato paste	4 oz.
Thyme	1½ tsp.
Allspice, ground	½ tsp.
Nutmeg, ground	½ tsp.
Bay leaf	2
Salt and black pepper	to taste

Raise heat to high, add the wine, and deglaze the pan. Add the beef stock, tomato paste, and seasonings. Bring to a boil, then add to the browned oxtails. Simmer for 1 hour. If more liquid is needed add a 50/50 mixture of red wine and beef stock. Adjust seasonings, if necessary, and continue to simmer for another 20–30 minutes, or until the meat is tender.

Serve in heated, deep plates with some of the cooking liquids. Accompany with rice and black beans.

KIDNEYS WITH SHERRY   *Puerto Rico*

Yield: 10 servings

Kidneys, beef or veal	5 lb.
Water	as needed
Vinegar, wine	as needed

Wash the kidneys, then cut each lengthwise into halves. Remove membrane and fat, place in a glass or stainless-steel container, and cover with a mixture of 2 parts water to 1 part vinegar. Refrigerate for at least 4 hours.

Flour	4 oz.
Thyme	1 tbsp.
Salt and black pepper	to taste

Combine the flour, thyme, salt, and pepper and blend thoroughly. Reserve.

Butter, clarified	as needed
Onions, sliced thin	4–5 oz.

To prepare an individual serving: Heat butter over medium to high heat. Sauté the onion until lightly browned. Remove the onion from the pan and reserve in a warm place.

(Continued)

Sherry, dry	2 – 3 oz.
Kidney	6 – 7 oz. per serving

Cut the kidney into bite-sized pieces and dredge in the flour mixture. Using the same pan, sauté the kidneys for a minute on each side. Add the sherry and simmer for several more minutes. Do not overcook. Place the kidneys on a warm plate surrounded by the reserved, fried onions. Spoon the pan liquids on top.

Serve with rice and fried plantains.

CURRIED GOAT   *Jamaica*

Yield: 10 – 12 servings

Marinade:

Onion, small dice	2 lb.
Corn oil	3 oz.
Curry powder	2 oz. or to taste
Salt	1 tbsp.
Pepper, coarsely ground	2 tsp.

Puree the onion, oil, and seasonings in a food processor using a steel blade. Set aside.

Goat meat, with bones	8 lb.

Trim meat and cut through the bone into serving-sized pieces. It is best to use a saw, as the bones have a tendency to splinter. Place the pieces in a glass or stainless-steel pan and rub the marinade over the meat. Cover and refrigerate for 4 – 6 hours or overnight.

Oil	as needed
Beef stock	as needed

In a heavy skillet, heat the oil and sauté the meat until browned on all sides. Transfer the pieces to a clean stew pot. Deglaze the skillet with a small amount of the beef stock and pour over the goat meat. Add any juices remaining in the pan used to marinate the meat and additional beef stock to just cover. Simmer for about 1 – 1½ hours, or until the meat is tender.

Potatoes, small dice	2–3 lb.

Cook potatoes in boiling water until just done. Cool and reserve. Add to meat prior to serving.

Accompany with mixed green salad.

COLD BEEF SALAD WITH AVOCADO   *Mexico*

Yield: 10–12 servings

Beef brisket, well trimmed	4–4½ lb.
Onion, quartered	1 lb.
Jalapeño, whole	1
Marjoram	1 tbsp.
Thyme	1 tsp.
Bay leaf	3
Salt	to taste
Black peppercorns	to taste

Place the brisket in enough cold water to cover. Bring to a rapid boil. Lower heat to medium and cook for 10–15 minutes, skimming liquid as needed. When broth is clear add the onion, jalapeño, and seasonings. Cover pot partially and simmer for 2 hours, or until the meat is very tender. Let cool in the broth. Remove meat and cut across the grain into 2-inch-wide strips. Using your fingers, shred the beef into strands. Strain and reserve the broth for other uses.

Olive oil	12 oz.
Vinegar, cider	4 oz.
Garlic, minced	1 tsp.
Salt	to taste
Black pepper, coarsely ground	to taste

Whisk together the oil, vinegar, garlic, salt, and pepper, pour over the shredded meat, and mix thoroughly. Reserve.

Potatoes, boiling, peeled and diced	1½ lb.

Cook the potatoes in boiling water until just tender. When done, place in ice water immediately. When cool, drain and add to the meat. Mix gently and reserve.

Romaine *or* other assertive green	as needed
Avocado slices	as needed
Queso fresco, feta, mozzarella, *or* other fresh white cheese	as needed
Chipotle chilies, cut in julienne	as needed
Green olives	as needed
Red radishes	as needed

To prepare an individual serving: Line a chilled plate with the lettuce leaves. Place a mound of the meat mixture in the center of the plate. Garnish with avocado slices, fresh cheese, chilies, green olives, and red radishes.

CHORIZO   *Mexico*

Yield: 6 lb.

Pork shoulder *or* a 50/50 mix of pork and beef	6 lb.

Cut the meat into pieces that can be easily fed into a meat grinder. Trim fat only if it is in excess of 1 lb. Grind the meat twice using a coarse plate, and place in a stainless-steel pan for mixing.

Garlic, minced	2 tbsp.
Hot pepper* flakes	2½ tsp. or to taste
Oregano, dried	1 tbsp.
Salt	2 tbsp.
Clove, ground	1½ tsp.
Cumin, ground	1½ tsp.
Black pepper, coarsely ground	2 tsp.
Paprika	3 oz.

In a separate mixing bowl combine the garlic and seasonings thoroughly.

*Other chili peppers, alone or in combination, may be used, such as dried ancho or pasillas, fresh, hot, finely minced peppers, or pure ground red chilies. Other flavoring agents may be adjusted to suit individual taste. For an interesting variation, add raisins and nuts, such as chopped, toasted peanuts, almonds, or pine nuts.

Vinegar	8 oz.
Water	as needed

Add the vinegar and water to the flavorings and mix into a thin paste. Distribute this mixture evenly over the ground meat, then blend thoroughly. (An electric mixer can also be used to combine these ingredients.) Cover meat and refrigerate overnight to let the flavors develop. Fry a teaspoon of the sausage and taste; adjust the seasonings if necessary.

Sausage casing	4 yd.

Soak the dry-packed casings in cold water for several hours; soak casings packed in brine for 1 hour. Run casings under cold water and cut out any holes or tears. Knot the casings at those points. Using an electric grinder with the cutting blades removed and the sausage-stuffer attachment in place, place a length of casing over the stuffing attachment. Tie a knot in the end of the casing. Refeed the sausage through the machine and into the casing. Twist or tie filled casings into links approximately 6 inches in length. Hang sausages in the refrigerator to dry for several days before using. Place a tray beneath the sausages to collect any excess liquid.

FAJITAS   *Mexico*

Yield: 10–12 servings

Marinade:

Lime juice	6 oz.
Tequila	4 oz.
Corn oil	2 oz.
Cornstarch	2 tsp.
Jalapeños, seeds and ribs removed; minced	2 whole
Garlic, minced	1 tbsp.
Cilantro leaves, chopped	10 sprigs
Salt	1 tsp.
Black pepper	1 tsp.

Combine these ingredients.

(Continued)

Beef flank steak	5 lb.

Trim flank steaks of all flat and membrane. Place in a shallow glass or stainless steel pan and cover with marinade. Cover pan and let marinate overnight or up to two days in the refrigerator. Turn meat occasionally.

Marinated meat	as needed 5 – 6 oz. per serving
Lime juice, fresh	as needed

Place meat on grill, or, preferably, over hot coals and grill until rare. Baste several times with the marinade while cooking. Remove from grill and slice thin across the grain. Heat a small, lightly oiled, iron skillet over high heat until just at the smoking point. To serve, place slices of meat on the hot skillet and add a tablespoon of fresh lime juice just prior to serving. Place hot skillet on a heat resistant liner and take directly to the table.

Top with thick slices of onion that have been sauteed over low heat until lightly browned. Serve with guacamole or diced avocado that has been tossed in fresh lemon juice, sour cream, tomato salsa, and re-fried beans. Accompany with a side dish of warm tortillas.

Chicken breast, cut into 1 inch strips, or peeled, raw shrimp may be used instead of beef. Marinate these products from 4 – 6 hours then thread appropriate amounts on skewers for individual portions. Grill, then serve in the same manner.

BEEF PIES WITH DRIED FRUITS   *Argentina*

Yield: 10 – 12 individual servings

Dried fruit(s)*	1 lb.
Wine, red dry	as needed

Place the dried fruit in a small stainless steel or glass bowl and add enough wine to just cover.

---

*Use any dried fruits such as raisins, prunes, or apricots. Fruits may be used singly or in combination.

Beef, tenderloin, trimmed	3½ lb.
Olive oil	as needed

Chill meat to just above freezing. This will enable you to cut the meat into very thin slices. In a large skillet, heat the oil to just below the smoking point and quickly sauté the sliced meat in small batches. When each batch is done, place in a bowl so that the juices will be retained. Reserve in a warm place.

Onion, sliced thin	1½ lb.
Red wine, dry	8 oz.

Using the same skillet, sauté the onions over low heat until they begin to brown. Raise heat, add the wine, and deglaze the pan.

Tomato paste	2 tbsp.
Oregano	1 tbsp.
Cinnamon, ground	1 tsp.
Allspice	1 tsp.
Salt and black pepper	to taste

Add these ingredients, lower heat, and simmer, uncovered, until the liquids have evaporated.

Reserved meat and meat juices	
Dried fruit(s)	
Pastry dough	as needed

Remove from heat and add the meat and dried fruit. Mix well. Divide into 10–12 equal portions and place in deep, oven proof, individual serving dishes. Meat and fruit should almost fill each dish. Cover tops of dishes with pastry dough. Cut a hole or other ornamental shapes in top of dough so that steam can be released while cooking. Reserve under refrigeration until needed.

Egg, beaten	as needed

To prepare an individual serving, bring dish to room temperature, brush top with beaten egg and place in a 375 degree F oven until golden brown.

Serve with cooked green vegetable or salad.

GOAT RAGOUT   *St. Thomas*

Yield: 10–12 servings

Goat meat in serving size pieces, bone in or bone out, in 1½ inch cubes	8 lb. (bone in) 5 lb. (bone out)
Papaya, seeds removed and sliced thin	3
Wine, red	16 oz.
Garlic, minced	1 tbsp.
Allspice, ground	2 tsp.

If using goat meat with the bone in, cut through all bones with a saw as they tend to splinter. Place meat in a stainless steel or glass pan layered with slices of papaya. Mix the wine, allspice, and garlic together and pour over the meat and papaya. Cover and refrigerate overnight.

Vegetable oil	3 oz.
Reserved goat meat	
Onion, diced	3 lb.
Green bell peppers, seeded and diced	3 lb.
Celery, sliced	4 oz.
Green chili peppers, seeded and minced	3 tsp. or to taste
Beef stock	as needed
Bay leaf	2

In a heavy skillet, heat the oil over medium to high heat. Remove meat from marinade, pat dry, and sauté until browned. Transfer meat to a clean casserole. Using the same skillet, sauté the onions and green bell peppers until soft. Add the celery, and chili peppers and continue to cook for another minute. Add the marinade and bring to a boil. Deglaze the skillet and pour contents over the goat meat in the casserole. Add stock to cover and the bay leaf, and simmer for 2 to 2½ hours or until the meat is tender. Let cool and refrigerate. Remove congealed fat and bay leaf. Reheat as needed.

Serve with batatas or any other starchy tuber and a cooked, green, leafy vegetable.

ROAST PORK   *Jamaica*

Yield: 10–12 servings

Pork loin, boned	5 lb.

Trim excess fat and tie with butcher's twine to ensure round, uniform slices.

Garlic, minced	1 tbsp.
Salt	2 tsp.
Black pepper	2 tsp.
Ginger, ground	2 tsp.
Clove, ground	1 tsp.
Oil, vegetable	as needed

Mix all ingredients except oil. Then add enough oil to bind ingredients and make a smooth paste. Rub mixture evenly over pork's entire surface.

Stock, chicken or veal	6 oz.
Rum, dark	4 oz.

Place pork on a rack set in a small roasting pan. Pour mixture of stock and rum into pan and roast in a 350 degree F oven for ½ hour.

Glaze:

Rum, dark	4 oz.
Lime or lemon juice	4 oz.
Sugar, brown	4 oz.

Dissolve the sugar in the rum and juice. Baste the pork with this mixture every 10 minutes. Roast pork for another 45 minutes or until internal temperature reaches 160 degrees. When done, remove meat, wrap loosely in aluminum foil, and set aside in a warm place.

Pan liquids	
Stock	if needed
Corn starch	4 tsp. or as needed
Water	4 oz. or as needed

Degrease the pan liquids and strain. Add stock to bring liquid volume to 24 oz. by adding stock or any unused basting mixture. Bring to a boil in a small sauce pan. Skim, if necessary. Dissolve a small amount of cornstarch in water. Lower heat to simmer, add the cornstarch and, stirring, simmer until the liquids thicken. Place a small pool of the sauce on a heated plate and arrange slices of pork on top. Serve with rice or fried plantains.

VEGETABLES AND SALADS

PLANTAIN CROQUETTES   *Cuba*

Yield: variable

Butter, whole	2 oz.
Flour, bread	3 oz.

Melt butter in a small, heavy saucepan over low to medium heat. Add flour, mix well, and cook for 5 minutes, stirring, to make a smooth roux. Do not allow the roux to color.

Chicken stock, cold	1 qt.

Add the cold stock and mix well using a wire whisk. Simmer, stirring frequently, until the liquid has been reduced by half. Reserve.

Green plantain puree (see the recipe later in this section)	2 lb.
Cilantro leaves, fresh, chopped	1 bunch
Salt and white pepper	to taste

Place the plantain puree in a mixing bowl and add the cilantro. Mix well. Add half of the white chicken sauce and mix well. Continue adding the sauce until the mixture is the proper texture for shaping small croquettes. Add salt and pepper. Cool mixture in refrigerator, covered, for several hours before shaping croquettes.

Flour	as needed
Eggs, beaten	as needed
Bread crumbs	as needed

Shape plantain mixture into croquettes approximately 2–3 inches long. (Other sizes and shapes may also be made.) Bread using standard breading procedure: flour, egg, and bread crumbs. Place on rack and refrigerate for several hours. Just prior to serving, deep-fry at 375 degrees F, drain, and serve with a tomato salsa. (See recipe.)

May also be served as a side dish for meat, fish, or chicken entrées.

POTATOES AND GREEN BEANS CHORREADAS   *Mexico*

Yield: 10–12 servings

Sauce:

Oil, olive *or* vegetable	1 oz.
Onions, small dice	1½ lb.
Jalapeños, seeded, ribs removed, and minced	4
Garlic, minced	1 tbsp.

In a small saucepan, heat oil over medium heat. Sauté the onions until soft. Add the peppers and garlic and cook for another minute.

Turmeric	1 tbsp.
Cumin, ground	2 tsp.
Ginger root, minced	2 tsp.

Add the seasonings, stir well, and continue to cook for another minute.

Tomatoes, peeled, seeded, and chopped	2½ lb.
Cilantro leaves, fresh, chopped	1 bunch

Add the tomatoes and cilantro and simmer for 30 minutes or until the mixture begins to thicken. Let cool and reserve.

Cheddar *or* Muenster, grated	as needed
Sour cream	as needed
New potatoes, boiled	as needed
Green beans, steamed	as needed

Prior to serving, reheat the sauce as needed. Add 1 tbsp. of cheese and 1 tbsp. of sour cream per serving. Place over low heat until the cheese has melted. Spoon over hot, boiled new potatoes and steamed green beans.

May be served as an appetizer or as a vegetable accompaniment for grilled meats or poultry.

JICAMA AND ORANGE SALAD   *Mexico*

Yield: 10–12 servings

Oranges (Navel, Valencia, *or* Temple)	6

Peel oranges, remove white membrane, and break into sections. Slice the sections into ¼-inch pieces. Place in a glass or stainless-steel mixing bowl. Reserve the juice separately.

Jicama	2½ lb.	Peel and dice the jicamas, keeping the pieces approximately the same size as the orange pieces. Add the jicama to the oranges.

Orange juice	as needed	Add enough orange juice to the reserved orange juice to make 8 oz. Add the oil and seasonings and mix well. Adjust seasonings to make a well-balanced mixture. Pour over the oranges and jicama.
Corn oil	2 oz.	
Cayenne pepper	to taste	
Salt	to taste	
Sugar	to taste	

Cilantro leaves, fresh, chopped	6 tbsp.	Add the cilantro and toss well. Refrigerate for 3–4 hours. Toss again before serving.

ZUCCHINI IN TOMATO CREAM SAUCE   *Mexico*

Yield: 10–12 servings

Zucchini *or other* summer squash	2½ lb.	Select small, uniform zucchini. Wash well then slice on the diagonal to make oval slices. Reserve.

Tomatoes, peeled, seeded, and chopped	2½ lb.	Combine the remaining ingredients in a heavy saucepan and, stirring occasionally, bring to a boil over low heat. Simmer for 25–30 minutes. Adjust seasonings, if necessary. Add the zucchini and simmer until tender.
Heavy cream	8 oz.	
Jalapeños, seeded, ribs removed, and minced	3	
Mint leaves, fresh, chopped	2 tbsp.	
Cilantro leaves, fresh chopped	2 tbsp.	
Cloves	1 tsp.	
Cinnamon, ground	½ tsp.	
Salt and black pepper	to taste	

ZUCCHINI WITH TOMATOES AND JALAPEÑOS   *Mexico*

Yield: 10–12 servings

Oil, olive *or* corn	2 oz.
Onion, chopped	8 oz.
Garlic, minced	2 tsp.
Jalapeño, seeded, ribs removed, and minced	1 or to taste

In a heavy saucepan, heat the oil over medium heat and sauté the onions until soft. Add the garlic and jalapeño pepper and sauté for another minute.

Tomatoes, peeled and chopped	2½ lb.
Cilantro leaves, fresh, chopped	5–6 sprigs
Salt and black pepper	to taste

Add the tomatoes and cilantro and simmer until the liquids begin to thicken. Adjust for salt and pepper. The dish may be prepared in advance up to this point.

Zucchini	2 lb.
Corn kernels	6 oz.

Prior to serving: Wash the zucchini, then grate using the large holes on a grater, cut into small dice, or slice thin. Place in a colander with a weight on top and allow to drain for 30 minutes. Cut the corn kernels from the cob. Bring the tomato sauce to a simmer and add the zucchini and corn. Cook for 3–5 minutes. If preparing individual servings, portion the grated zucchini and corn accordingly.

AVOCADO SALAD WITH ORANGE AND ONION   *Caribbean*

Yield: 10–12 servings

Dressing:

Olive oil	3 parts
Vinegar	2 parts
Tabasco sauce	to taste
Salt and black pepper	to taste

Combine the oil, vinegar, and seasonings and whisk until blended.

Salad:

Avocado, sliced, in strips	as needed
Lemon juice	as needed
Romaine *or* other salad greens, cut in julienne	as needed
Orange slices	as needed
Onion, red, sliced thin	as needed
Olives, green, pimiento stuffed, sliced	as needed

Place the sliced avocado in a glass or stainless-steel bowl and toss with the lemon juice. Place a bed of lettuce on a chilled salad plate and arrange the avocado slices in an attractive pattern in the center. Arrange the orange slices and the onions around the avocado, then distribute the sliced olives on top of the oranges and onions. Spoon the dressing over the salad.

AVOCADO WITH PEPPERS AND TOMATOES *Colombia*

Yield: 10–12 servings

Avocado pulp	1½ lb.
Lemon juice, fresh squeezed	as needed

Peel and dice the avocado and toss in lemon juice. Reserve in refrigerator.

Bacon, slab, small dice	¾ lb.

Sauté the bacon until very crisp. Remove from skillet and reserve. Discard rendered fat.

Tomatoes, peeled, seeded, and chopped	1 lb.
Onion, diced	1 lb.
Green bell pepper, seeded and diced	½ lb.
Jalapeños, seeds removed	3
Garlic, minced	2 tsp.
Olive oil	as needed

Place the vegetables in the bowl of a food processor and puree until smooth. In the skillet used to fry the bacon, heat the olive oil over moderate heat and simmer the puree for 10 minutes, stirring frequently.

(Continued)

Vinegar, white wine	4–5 oz. or to taste	Add vinegar and salt and let cool. Gently fold the reserved avocado into the mixture. When serving, garnish with the bacon bits.
Salt	to taste	

FRIED PLANTAINS   *Caribbean*   Yield: 2–3 oz. per serving

Plantains, ripe or half ripe	as needed	Peel the plantains and make diagonal slices ½- to 1-inch thick. Place in ice water for 30 minutes. Drain and pat dry.
Vegetable oil	as needed	The plantains may be deep-fried at a temperature of 350–375 degrees F or pan-fried. If panfried, turn once after one side is golden brown. Remove from oil with a slotted spoon and drain on paper towels before serving.

Fried plantains are most often served with a sprinkling of salt and lemon juice. Other seasonings such as cayenne pepper or ground ginger may also be used. Cassava root may also be cooked in this manner. Serve as an appetizer, or as a side dish with beans and rice or meat and fish entrées.

Tostones are made by the same method. Use green plantains cut 1-inch thick on the diagonal. When slightly cool place a towel on top and flatten to half the original thickness. Return to the hot oil until golden brown. Remove and drain once again.

CREAMED CORN   *Mexico*   Yield: 10–12 servings

Corn, fresh	10 ears	Clean corn and cook in briskly boiling water for 4–6 minutes. When done, plunge corn into ice water, let cool, then cut the kernels from the cob. Reserve.
Butter, whole	2 oz.	In a heavy saucepan, heat butter over low heat and sauté the onion until soft. Add the chilies and tomatoes. Continue to cook over low heat until the tomatoes are soft.
Onion, minced	8 oz.	
Poblano chilies, roasted, peeled, seeded, ribs removed, and cut julienne	4–5	
Tomato, peeled and chopped	2 lb.	

Cream cheese, small cubes	12 oz.
Light cream *or* half & half	4 oz.
Salt and pepper	to taste

Add the cream cheese and cook until the cheese melts. Add the half & half, salt, and pepper and simmer for 5 minutes. Add the reserved corn and simmer for 1 or 2 minutes more.

CABBAGE WITH TOMATOES AND CHILIES *Bolivia*

Yield: 10–12 servings

White cabbage, shredded fine	2 lb.

Blanche the cabbage in boiling water until just tender. Drain and plunge immediately in ice water. The cabbage should be tender but still crisp. Reserve.

Potatoes, boiling	1 lb.

Peel and dice the potatoes and cook in boiling water until tender. Drain and plunge immediately in ice water. Reserve.

Vegetable oil	2 oz.
Onion, diced	¾ lb.
Tomatoes, peeled, seeded, and chopped	1½ lb.
Serrano chilies, seeded, ribs removed, and minced	2–3 or to taste
Cilantro leaves, fresh, chopped	4 tbsp.
Salt and black pepper	to taste

Heat the oil over moderate heat and sauté the onion until soft. Add the remaining ingredients and simmer for 20 minutes. Adjust for salt and pepper.

Combine the cabbage and potatoes with the other ingredients. Mix well. Reheat as needed.

SPINACH WITH HOT PEPPER AND TOMATOES   *Peru*

Yield: 10–12 servings

Oil, olive *or* corn	2 oz.
Onion, coarsely chopped	12 oz.
Garlic, minced	2 tsp.
Jalapeño, seeded, ribs removed, and minced	1 or to taste

In a heavy saucepan, heat the oil over medium heat and sauté the onion until soft. Add the garlic and jalapeño and sauté for another minute.

Tomatoes, peeled and chopped	2½ lb.
Salt and black pepper	to taste

Add the tomatoes and cook until the liquid begins to thicken. Adjust for salt and pepper. The recipe may be prepared in advance up to this point.

Spinach, washed and trimmed	4 lb.
Lemon zest	2 tsp.

Prior to serving, bring the tomato/onion mixture to a boil and add the spinach and lemon zest. Cook only until the spinach has wilted. Mix well before serving.

ZUCCHINI IN TOMATO CREAM SAUCE   *Mexico*

Yield: 10–12 servings

Butter	2 oz.
Tomatoes, peeled, seeded, and chopped	1½ lb.
Jalapeño, seeded, ribs removed, and minced	1
Cilantro leaves, chopped fine	4 tbsp.
Mint leaves, chopped fine	4 tbsp.
Clove, ground	½ tsp.
Cinnamon stick	2 inch
Salt and white pepper	to taste

Heat butter in a small saucepan over low to medium heat. When melted add the vegetables, herbs, and seasonings. Bring to boil, then lower heat and simmer for 30 minutes, partially covered.

Heavy cream	12 oz.

Add cream and simmer for 15 minutes. Let cool and reserve. Remove cinnamon stick.

Zucchini *or* other summer squash, trimmed and cut into ¼-inch rounds	2½ lb.

To prepare an individual serving: Place 2–3 oz. of the tomato/cream sauce in a small pan. Add 3–4 oz. of the squash. Simmer, covered, for 3–4 minutes, or until the squash is just tender but not overcooked.

SHREDDED KALE   *Brazil*

Yield: 10–12 servings

Kale*	3 lb.
Water, boiling	1 qt.
Water, ice	as needed

Trim the tough stem ends from the kale. Using a vegetable peeler, peel the backs of remaining stems. Cutting across the stems, slice the kale into very fine strips. Place the kale in the boiling water and cook for 2–3 minutes. Remove the kale and plunge it immediately into ice water. When cool, drain, cover, and refrigerate until needed.

Lard, bacon fat, *or* oil	as needed
Egg, hard cooked, chopped	as needed

To prepare an individual serving: Heat fat in a skillet over medium heat. Add 4 oz. of kale and sauté quickly, stirring, until the kale is heated through. Garnish with hard cooked, chopped egg.

*Collard greens or chickory may be substituted.

JICAMA AND TANGERINE SALAD   *Mexico*

Yield: 10–12 servings

Jicama root	2 lb.
Apple, cubed	1 lb.
Grapefruit juice, fresh squeezed	4 oz.
Lime juice, fresh squeezed	4 oz.
Salt	as needed

Use small jicama roots weighing no more than 1 lb. each. Peel and cut into ½-inch cubes. Place in a glass or stainless-steel bowl with the cubed apple. Add the fruit juices and sprinkle with a little salt. Toss well, cover, and let marinate, refrigerated, for 2–3 hours.

(Continued)

Romaine leaves	as needed
Cantaloupe, peeled and cubed (same size as the jicama)	as needed
Tangerine, sections, seeds removed	as needed
Cilantro leaves, fresh, chopped	as needed
Chili powder, mild	as needed

To prepare an individual serving: Place a bed of romaine on a chilled salad plate. In a small mixing bowl place 4–5 oz. of the jicama and apple, several ounces of cantaloupe, and a few spoonfuls of the marinated fruit juices. Mix well and place a mound in the center of the plate. Garnish with a ring of tangerine slices. Sprinkle with chopped, fresh cilantro leaves and a small amount of chili powder.

STEWED OKRA AND POTATOES   *Caribbean*

Yield: 10–12 servings

Achiote oil (see the recipe in the "Regional Flavorings" section)	3 tbsp.
Slab bacon, small dice	4 oz.

In a heavy saucepan, heat the achiote oil and sauté the bacon until all of the fat has been rendered. Remove the bacon bits and reserve.

Onion, large dice	1 lb.
Tomatoes, peeled, seeded, and chopped	2 lb.
Green bell pepper, seeded and chopped	8 oz.
Cilantro leaves, fresh chopped	6 tbsp.
Salt and black pepper	to taste

Sauté the onion in the achiote oil and rendered bacon fat until soft. Add the tomatoes, peppers, and cilantro. Cook over low heat for another 15–20 minutes. Add salt and pepper.

Okra	2 lb.
Potatoes, cooked, peeled, and cubed	2 lb.

Use small, whole okra if possible. If not, trim stem ends and chop. Add the okra to the pot along with enough water to barely cover. Bring to a boil, then lower heat and simmer for 20–30 minutes. Add the potatoes, mix gently, and heat through.

Serve as an accompaniment for fish and meat entrées.

SALAD CARIOCA   *Brazil*

Yield: 10 servings

Grapefruit	5

Using a serrated knife, cut a slice just thick enough to expose the flesh from the top and bottom of each grapefruit. Starting at the top, cut away the remaining zest, pith, and skin following the curve of the fruit. Working over a bowl to catch the juices, section the fruit by cutting along the membranes separating each section. Cut the sections into bite-sized pieces and remove seeds. Place the grapefruit pieces in a glass or stainless-steel bowl. Reserve the juice separately.

Cucumber	2 lb.

Peel the cucumber, then slice lengthwise. Remove seeds using a spoon. Slice crosswise into very thin slices and add to the grapefruit pieces.

Grapefruit juice	8 oz.
Sugar	2 oz. or to taste
Oil, corn *or* light olive	2 oz.
Mint leaves, fresh, chopped fine	4 tbsp.
Jalapeño, seeded, ribs removed, and minced	1
Salt	½ tsp.
Radicchio *or* lettuce of choice	as needed

Add additional grapefruit juice to the reserved juice to make 8 oz. Add the remaining ingredients and stir until the sugar is completely dissolved. Pour over the grapefruit and cucumber and toss well. Refrigerate for 1–2 hours before serving. Serve on a bed of radicchio on a chilled salad plate.

PUMPKIN SOUFFLÉ   *Brazil*

Yield: 10–12 servings

Pumpkin	3½ lb. (to make approximately 2½ lb. puree)

Wash pumpkin and cut in half. Remove all strings and seeds. Place pumpkin cut side down on a lightly oiled sheet pan and bake at 350 degrees F for 40–50 minutes, or until it softens and the shell begins to collapse. Remove from oven and let cool. When cool enough to handle,

(Continued)

scrape out the pulp and puree in a food processor fitted with a steel blade. An alternate method is to cut the pumpkin into manageable pieces, discard the strings and seeds, peel away the skin, and cut the flesh into cubes. Place in boiling water and cook until tender. When done, drain well, press to remove excess moisture, then puree.

Eggs, separated	4	Beat yolks with 1 tbsp. of water. Reserve. Beat whites until stiff but not dry. Reserve.
Butter, whole, sweet	6 oz.	Add the egg yolks, butter, heavy cream, and seasonings to the pumpkin puree and mix well.
Heavy cream	4 oz.	
Nutmeg, ground	½ tsp. or to taste	
Salt and white pepper	to taste	
Butter	as needed	Fold in the egg whites, then pour into buttered ramekins for individual servings, or into a larger baking dish for buffet service. Sprinkle top with cheese. Bake in a 350 degree F oven until firm and a toothpick or skewer inserted in the center comes out clean. (Cooking time will vary, depending on the utensil used.)
Swiss cheese, grated	as needed	

Serve with meat or poultry entrées.

PLANTAINS WITH MOLASSES   *Panama*

Yield: 10–12 servings

Butter	¼ lb.	In a heavy sauté pan, heat butter until foamy. Add the plantains and brown on each side. When done, place in a single layer in a glass or stainless-steel baking dish.
Plantains, ripe, peeled and cut into 4 pieces each	6 large*	

---

*If smaller plantains are used, calculate 4 oz. per serving after peel has been removed.

Molasses	12 oz.
Water	16 oz.
Cinnamon stick	3 in.
Cloves	1 tsp.
Salt	½ tsp.

Using the same pan, add the molasses, water, cinnamon stick, cloves, and salt. Bring to a boil, then lower heat and simmer for 15 minutes. Remove the cinnamon stick and cloves. Pour this mixture over the sautéed plantains.

Butter	as needed

Dot lightly with butter. Cover with foil and bake in a 350 degree F oven until the plantains are soft. (Cooking time will vary, depending on the ripeness of the plantains.)

Served as an accompaniment for meat, poultry, and rice dishes.

GUACAMOLE WITH ZUCCHINI   *Mexico*

Yield: 10–12 servings

Zucchini, grated	1½ lb.
Tomatoes, peeled, seeded, and chopped	1½ lb.
Scallions, white and tender green parts, sliced thin	6
Jalapeños, seeded, ribs removed, and minced	2 or to taste

Press zucchini gently to remove excess liquid. Then mix the vegetables thoroughly.

Olive oil	6 oz.
Lime juice, fresh squeezed	4 oz.
Salt and black pepper	to taste

Mix the oil, lime juice, salt, and pepper, then add to the vegetables and toss well. Cover and refrigerate until needed.

(Continued)

Avocado, small	½ per serving
Lettuce	as needed

Just prior to serving, prepare the avocado, which may be sliced, cut into cubes, or removed from the shell with a melon ball scoop. Place 4–5 oz. per serving of the reserved salad in a mixing bowl. Add the avocado and toss well to coat with the oil and lime dressing. On a chilled salad plate, place a mound of the salad on a bed of lettuce.

GREEN PLANTAIN PUREE   *Panama*

Yield: 10–12 servings

Green plantains	4 lb.*

Cut off about ¼ inch from the tips of the plantains, then slit the peel lengthwise on opposite sides of the fruit. Place unpeeled plantains in enough cold water to cover. Bring to a boil, then cook over medium heat for 25–30 minutes, or until the plantains can be easily pierced with a fork. Drain and reserve until cool enough to handle. Peel and place in the bowl of a food processor fitted with a steel blade.

Butter, cut in small pieces	4 oz.
Milk, hot	approximately 8 oz.
Salt and white pepper	to taste

Add the butter, turn on the processor, then slowly add the milk until a smooth, firm puree has resulted. The amount of milk needed will vary.

Serve as an accompaniment for meat, chicken, or fish entrées.

---

*Peelings will result in approximately 20 percent weight loss. An average portion size is 4–5 oz.

CORN SALAD *Mexico*

Yield: 10 – 12 servings

Corn, fresh, on the cob	10 – 12 ears
Red bell peppers, seeded, roasted, peeled, then chopped	1 lb.
Green bell pepper, seeded, roasted, peeled, then chopped	8 oz.
Tomatoes, peeled and chopped	1 lb.
Onion, minced	4 oz.
Parsley leaves, fresh, chopped	4 tbsp.

Shuck corn, then place in a pot of rapidly boiling water for 3 – 5 minutes, or until the kernels are just tender. Cut the kernels from the cob and place in a mixing bowl. Add the vegetables and parsley and mix well.

Oil, olive or vegetable	6 oz.
Vinegar	2 oz.
Oregano, dried	2 tsp.
Salt and black pepper	to taste

Combine the oil, vinegar, and seasonings and mix well. Pour over corn salad and toss to coat evenly. Cover and refrigerate at least 2 hours before serving.

STEWED CORN AND CHAYOTE *Costa Rica*

Yield: 10 – 12 servings

Corn on cob	8 ears
Chayote	5

Cut the kernels from the cobs and reserve. Peel the chayote, cut into small cubes, and reserve.

Butter, clarified	4 tbsp.
Onion, chopped	4 oz.
Garlic, minced	2 tsp.

Heat butter in a large skillet over medium heat. Sauté the onions until soft. Add the garlic and cook for another minute.

Add the reserved corn and chayote and sauté over high heat stirring, for 1 – 2 minutes.

(Continued)

Cilantro leaves, fresh, chopped	4 tbsp.
Salt	to taste
Sugar	to taste
Milk	as needed

Add the cilantro leaves, salt, sugar, and milk; the milk should barely cover the vegetables. Simmer, uncovered, for 5–6 minutes.

Serve individual portions in small warmed bowls with meat or poultry entrées.

MEXICAN-STYLE CAULIFLOWER

Yield: 10–12 servings

Sauce:

Oil, olive *or* vegetable	1 oz.
Onion, minced	8 oz.
Tomatoes, peeled, seeded, and chopped	2 lb.
Olives, green, pitted and chopped	2 oz.
Parsley, flat leaf, chopped	3 tbsp.
Capers	2 tsp.
Cinnamon	1 tsp.
Sugar	1 tsp.
Salt and black pepper	to taste

In a small saucepan, heat the oil over medium to low heat and sauté the onions until soft. Add the tomatoes, olives, parsley, capers, and seasonings and simmer, partially covered, for 15–20 minutes. Adjust seasonings, if necessary. Let cool and reserve until needed.

Cauliflower	2½ lb.

Remove core and outer leaves, then cut into uniform florets. Blanche or steam florets until barely tender. Do not overcook. When done, plunge the cauliflower immediately into ice water. Reserve until needed.

Bread crumbs	as needed
Monterey Jack *or* sharp Cheddar, grated	as needed
Oil	as needed

To prepare an individual serving: Place 3 oz. of the cauliflower and 2 oz. of the tomato sauce into an individual-serving, heatproof dish. Sprinkle the top lightly with bread crumbs, grated cheese, and a little oil. Place in a 425 degree F oven until the top begins to brown.

CAULIFLOWER WITH ALMONDS   *Chile*

Yield: variable

Béchamel Sauce:
Yield: 1 quart

Butter, sweet, whole	2 oz.
Flour, bread	3 oz.

In a small, heavy saucepan, melt the butter over medium to low heat. Add the flour and mix well. Cook over low heat, stirring occasionally, for 3–4 minutes. Allow to cool.

Milk, scalded	1 qt.
Onion, minced	4 oz.
Nutmeg	to taste

Using a wire whisk, gradually add the milk to the roux. When the milk and roux are well blended, add the onion and simmer for 25–30 minutes. Add nutmeg to taste. Option: For a smoother consistency, strain the sauce at this point.

Almonds, ground	4 oz.
Salt and white pepper	to taste

Add the almonds, salt, and pepper. The sauce should have a fairly thick consistency. Simmer for another 5 minutes.

Cauliflower florets	3 oz. per serving

Trim and cut cauliflower into bite-sized florets. Steam or boil as needed, until just tender. Spoon warm béchamel on top.

Serve with any grilled meat, poultry, or fish entrée.

BREADED BANANAS   *Brazil*   Yield: 1 serving

Banana, small*	1
Flour	as needed
Egg, beaten	as needed
Bread crumbs	as needed

Cut banana in half lengthwise. Use standard breading procedure: flour, egg, and bread crumbs, to coat.

Butter *or* vegetable oil	as needed

Sauté the breaded banana on both sides until golden brown.

Serve as a side dish with meats.

BATATA CROQUETTES
Caribbean

Yield: 10–12 servings

Batatas**	4 lb.

Peel, slice, and cook batatas in boiling water until tender. Place in the bowl of an electric mixer fitted with a wire whisk. (When working with batatas, drop them in cold water immediately after cutting as the flesh has a tendency to discolor quickly.)

Butter, whole	4 oz.
Onion, small	8 oz.

In a small sauté pan, heat the butter over low heat. Add the onion and sauté until soft but do not brown. Add this to the batatas.

Eggs, beaten	4
Milk	4 oz.
Flour	2 oz.
Salt	2 tsp. or to taste
White pepper	1 tsp. or to taste
Oil *or* butter	as needed

Add the eggs, milk, flour, salt, and pepper to the mixing bowl and blend thoroughly on medium speed. Sauté a teaspoon of the mixture in a little oil or butter. Adjust seasonings if necessary.

---

*If bananas are large, use only half per serving. Plantains may also be prepared in this manner.
**Batata is also known as boniato, white sweet potato, and camote, and may be served boiled or baked.

Bread crumbs, dry	as needed	Form the batata mixture into balls or rounded ovals. Dredge in the bread crumbs to coat all surfaces. Place on a rack and refrigerate for several hours before deep-frying at 375 degrees F.

Serve 2–3, depending on size, with fish, poultry, or meat entrées.

CORN PUDDING   *Colombia*

Yield: 10–12 servings

Corn	10 ears	Cut the kernels from the cob and place them in a mixing bowl.
Eggs, beaten	6	Combine these ingredients, then add to the corn kernels and mix well.
Milk	12 oz.	
Corn oil	2 oz.	
Salt	1–2 tsp. or to taste	
Paprika, Spanish	2 tsp.	
White pepper	1 tsp. or to taste	
Butter	as needed	Butter, then flour a small baking dish. Invert dish and remove excess flour. Pour half of the corn mixture into the baking dish. Top with a layer of thinly sliced cheese. Pour remaining corn mixture on top. Place in a pan of hot water reaching halfway up the sides of the corn pudding and bake at 350 degrees F until set.
Flour	as needed	
Cheese, fresh mozzarella	as needed	

For single portion servings, timbales may be used.

BRASILIA SALAD   *Brazil*

Yield: as needed

Apples	in equal	Peel, core, and cut apples into thin slices.
Oranges	amounts	Prepare oranges in sections with the white
Bananas		membrane removed. Peel, and cut bananas lengthwise, then slice into half rounds.

(Continued)

Brazil nuts, slivered	1/8 volume of fruit
Orange juice	as needed

Toss fruits in a small amount of orange juice (enough to coat). Add the nuts and mix well.

Mayonnaise	as needed
Heavy cream, whipped	as needed
Salt and white pepper	to taste
Sugar	to taste

Combine the mayonnaise and whipped cream in equal parts. Add salt, white pepper, and sugar to taste. Add enough of this mixture to bind the fruit and nuts together. Chill well before serving.

Serve on a bed of assertive greens or watercress.

POTATO PANCAKES   *Ecuador*   Yield: variable

Onions, chopped	1 lb.
Butter, whole	2 oz.

Chop onions finely. Heat butter in a heavy skillet until it foams. Add the onions and saute, over low heat, until the onions are very soft and begin to color.

Potatoes, boiling	5 lb.

Boil potatoes in the skins until they can be easily pierced with a fork. Drain, and, when cool enough to handle, peel and mash. This can be done by hand or in an electric mixer fitted with a wire whisk.

Sauteed onions	
Cheese, munster or fresh mozzarella	8 oz.
Salt and white pepper	to taste

Add these ingredients and mix well. Potato mixture may be shaped in a variety of ways and sizes.* Chill well before using.

Lard, vegetable or achiote oil	as needed

To serve, saute potato cakes in hot oil until golden on both sides.

Serve with fried fish entrees. As a luncheon entree, top with fried eggs and garnish with lettuce, tomatoes, avocado, or other garden vegetables.

---

*Small balls for hors d'oeuvres, flat pancakes of differing sizes if served as an accompaniment to an entree, or as an entree.

POTATOES WITH TOMATO AND CHEESE SAUCE   *Colombia*

Yield: 10–12 servings

Sauce:

Butter, whole	2 oz.
Onions, chopped	1 lb.
Tomatoes, peeled, seeded, and chopped	2 lb.
Garlic, minced	½ tsp.

In a small sauce pan, heat the butter until it foams. Add the onions and saute until soft. Add the tomatoes and garlic and continue to cook, over low heat, until most of the liquids have evaporated.

Heavy cream	8 oz.
Cheese, grated, Muenster or fresh mozzarella	4 oz.
Salt and pepper	to taste

Add the cream and bring to a boil, stirring. When the cream has come to a boil, lower heat and add the cheese. Cook, over low heat, until the cheese has melted. Add salt and pepper to taste.

Potatoes, peeled and boiled	as needed

To serve, pour sauce over hot, boiled potatoes. Use 5–6 oz. of potatoes per serving.

DESSERTS

FRUIT EMPANADAS
South America

Yield: approximately 30 empanadas

Dough:

Plantains, green, unpeeled	5 lb.	Peel the plantains and place in enough boiling water to cover. Cook over medium heat for 30–40 minutes, or until the plantains are tender and their skins can be pierced easily. Drain, and when just cool enough to handle, place in the bowl of a food processor fitted with a steel blade.
Butter, whole, sweet	4 oz.	Add the butter, lemon zest, sugar, and allspice and pulse until smooth.
Lemon zest	1 tbsp.	
Sugar	1–2 oz.	
Allspice	½ tsp.	
Egg yolks	5	Add the egg yolks and blend thoroughly. Add enough flour to bind the ingredients into a smooth dough. Remove the plantain dough from the processor bowl and dust lightly with flour. Place in a clean bowl, cover, and let rest for 30 minutes.
Flour	as needed	

Filling:

Rum, dark	6 oz.	Place the rum, raisins, and cayenne in a glass or stainless-steel container and soak for 1 hour, or until the raisins become plump.
Raisins, golden	4 oz.	
Cayenne pepper	½ tsp.	
Fruit (Apples: Granny Smith, Cortland, Rome Beauty; pears: Bartlett, Red Bartlett, Bosc), used individually or in combination	3–3½ lb.	Peel and core the fruit. Take half the fruit and chop fine. Cut the remaining fruit into ½-inch cubes and reserve in water containing a small amount of lemon juice to prevent discoloring.
Water	as needed	
Lemon juice	as needed	

(Continued)

Butter, whole, sweet	2 oz.
Sugar, brown	8 oz.
Ginger root, minced	2 tsp.
Lemon zest	1 lemon
Cinnamon	½ tsp.
Water	12 oz.

In a stainless-steel saucepan, heat butter over medium heat until foamy. Add the sugar and cook, stirring, until the sugar has melted. Add the chopped fruit (reserving the cubed fruit), ginger root, lemon zest, cinnamon, and water and bring to a boil. Lower heat and simmer, stirring, until the mixture thickens and the water has evaporated.

Orange juice	4 oz.

Add the rum-soaked raisins, any remaining rum in the bowl, and the orange juice, mix well, and cook, stirring occasionally, for another 5–6 minutes, or until the mixture has thickened and the liquids have evaporated.

Walnuts, chopped	6 oz.

Add the cubed fruit and walnuts and cook for another 2–3 minutes. Remove from heat and let cool.

Assembly:

Egg and water, beaten	1 egg/2 tbsp. water
Sugar, confectioner's	as needed

Turn out the dough on a lightly floured surface and roll thin. Cut into 4-inch squares. Place the filling off-center and ½ inch from the edge. Using a pastry brush, lightly moisten the edges of the square. Fold over, corner to corner, to make a triangular shape. Pinch edges together. Make an attractive pattern on the sealed edge using the tines of a fork, spoon tip, or your fingers. Deep-fry at 375 degrees F, or brush with beaten egg and bake in a 350 degree F oven until golden. Dust with confectioner's sugar just before serving.

These empanadas may be made well in advance, tightly wrapped, frozen, and deep-fried directly from the freezer.

BANANA AU RHUM FLAMBÉ   *Haiti*

Yield: 1 serving

Banana, ripe but firm	1
Butter, melted	1 tbsp.
Sugar, brown	1 heaping tsp.

Peel and split the banana in half lengthwise. Place the melted butter in an individual-serving, ovenproof dish and add the banana. Turn the banana once to coat with butter on both sides. Sprinkle with brown sugar and place in a 450 degree F oven for 10 minutes, or until the banana is hot.

Lemon juice	as needed
Rum, dark, warmed	1 oz.

Add a sprinkling of lemon juice and return to the oven for 1–2 minutes. Just prior to serving, add the warmed rum and ignite. This can be done tableside if desired. Serve immediately when flames subside.

PEACHES POACHED WITH CHILI AND GINGER   *Peru*

Yield: 10 servings

Sugar	10 oz.
Water	1½ qt.
Chili pepper, hot, red, dried	1–2 small
Ginger root, peeled and sliced ¼-inch thick	2-inch piece
Saffron	pinch
Cloves, whole	1 tsp.

Combine the sugar, water, and spices in a stainless-steel saucepan and bring to a boil. Lower heat and simmer, uncovered, for 30 minutes.

Peaches, Freestones, unripe	10

Peel peaches and slice in half. Add peach halves to the poaching liquid. Simmer for 10–15 minutes, or until the peaches are tender. (Cooking time will vary depending on the ripeness of the fruit.) When done, transfer the

(Continued)

peach halves to a stainless-steel or glass pan and arrange them in a single layer. Increase the heat under the poaching liquid and reduce to 3 cups. Strain the syrup over the peaches, discarding the chili peppers, ginger root, and cloves. Reserve under refrigeration. Serve two peach halves per portion along with a small amount of the syrup.

PLANTAINS BAKED WITH CREAM   *Honduras*

Yield: 12 servings

Heavy cream	12 oz.
Sugar, brown	8 oz.
Cinnamon stick	3 – 4 inch piece

In a heavy-bottomed saucepan, combine the heavy cream, sugar, and cinnamon and bring to a boil over medium heat, stirring frequently. Lower heat and simmer for 10 minutes, stirring occasionally. Adjust sugar to taste. When done, remove the cinnamon stick and discard. Set cream mixture aside.

Plantains, ripe	six 8 – 10-oz. plantains
Butter, whole	as needed

Peel each plantain and slice lengthwise, then slice each half into thirds. Melt butter in a skillet, and sauté the plantains on both sides over medium heat until lightly browned. When done, transfer to a glass or stainless-steel baking dish. Arrange the plantains in a single layer and pour the cream mixture on top. Bake uncovered in a 350 degree F oven for 15 – 20 minutes. Serve warm or at room temperature.

PEACH AND CHERRY COMPOTE   *Guatemala*

Yield: 10 – 12 servings

Water	1 qt.
Sugar	8 oz.
Cinnamon stick	3 – 4-inch piece
Cloves, whole	1 tsp.

Combine the water, sugar, cinnamon, and cloves in a saucepan large enough to hold the fruits. Bring to a boil, then lower heat and simmer for 15 minutes. Remove the cinnamon stick and cloves and discard. Set syrup aside.

Peaches	4 lb.
Cherries	1 lb.

Peel the peaches, remove pits, and slice. Remove pits from cherries. Add fruit to syrup and simmer for 5 minutes. Let cool, then refrigerate until needed. Serve fruit, along with some of the syrup, in chilled goblets.

RICE PUDDING FLAVORED WITH BRANDY   *Mexico*

Yield: 10 – 12 servings

Raisins	4 oz.
Brandy	2 – 3 oz.

In a glass bowl, combine the raisins and brandy. Reserve.

Rice, long grain	1 lb.
Milk	1¼ qt.

In a heavy-bottomed saucepan, combine the rice and milk. Cover, then bring to a boil over moderate heat. Lower heat immediately and simmer, covered, until the rice is tender. An alternate method is to place the covered saucepan in a 350 degree F oven after the milk has boiled. Total cooking time is approximately 15 minutes.

Milk	1 pt.
Evaporated milk	12 oz.
Sugar	6 oz.
Cinnamon stick	2-inch piece
Vanilla	1 tbsp.
Salt	½ tsp.

In another heavy-bottomed saucepan, combine the milks, sugar, cinnamon, vanilla, and salt and bring to a boil over moderate heat. Lower heat immediately and simmer for 10 minutes. Remove the cinnamon stick and discard.

Cinnamon, powdered	as needed

Combine the reserved raisins and brandy with the cooked rice and the flavored milk mixture in the previous step. Mix well and simmer for 5 minutes, stirring occasionally. Adjust seasonings to taste. Portion the rice pudding in individual-serving dishes and chill. Dust lightly with powdered cinnamon just prior to serving.

MANGOES WITH CREM   *Jamaica*

Yield: 10 servings

Mangoes, fresh, pitted, and peeled	1½ lb. flesh

A 12-oz. mango will yield 4–5 oz. of flesh after the pit and peel have been removed. Place the mango flesh in the bowl of a food processor fitted with a steel blade. Use the pulse action to make a coarse puree.

Sugar	8 oz. or to taste
Rum	4 oz.
Lime juice, fresh squeezed	2 oz.

In a separate mixing bowl, combine the sugar, rum, and lime juice. Mix until the sugar is dissolved. Add the mango to this mixture and stir until all ingredients are thoroughly combined. Adjust sugar. Since it will be combined with unsweetened cream later, the mixture should be rather sweet.

Heavy cream, whipped	as needed

To serve, fold equal parts of the mango mixture with the whipped cream and place in chilled goblets. Do not overmix; retain some visible separation between the two products. Serve immediately.

BAKED BANANAS WITH ORANGE AND COCONUT   *Brazil*

Yield: 12 servings

Bananas (not overripe)	12
Butter, sweet	as needed

Peel bananas and cut in half lengthwise. Place in a buttered baking dish.

Orange juice, fresh squeezed	8 oz.
Lemon juice, fresh squeezed	2 oz.
Sugar, brown	4 oz.
Salt	½ tsp.
Butter, sweet	as needed

In a small saucepan, warm the orange and lemon juices. Add the sugar and stir to dissolve thoroughly; pour this mixture over the bananas. Dot with butter and place in a 400 degree F oven for 10 minutes.

Coconut, grated	as needed

Top with grated coconut before serving.

BAKED BANANAS WITH SHERRY   *Caribbean*

Yield: 10 servings

Orange juice	8 oz.
Sherry, dry	8 oz.
Sugar, brown	3 oz.
Butter, whole	2 oz.
Cinnamon	¾ tsp.
Nutmeg	½ tsp.

Combine the juice, sherry, sugar, butter, and spices over low heat, stirring, until the sugar has fully dissolved. Let cool.

Bananas*	10 medium

Peel the bananas and cut them in half lengthwise. Place in individual-serving, ovenproof dishes. Distribute the sauce equally over the bananas. Cover and reserve.

Rum	as needed

To prepare an individual serving: Place a sauced banana in a 450 degree F oven and bake, uncovered, for 10–15 minutes, or until the bananas are soft. Sprinkle with a little rum just prior to serving.

CHOCAO   *Panama*

Yield: 12 servings

Coconut milk, thin	3 pt.
Plaintains, very ripe, peeled	12

In a heavy saucepan, bring the coconut milk to a boil. Cut the plantains into pieces, add to the heated mixture, and cook over medium heat until the plantains are very soft. Remove from heat and mash the plantains together with the coconut milk.

(Continued)

*This step may be omitted and the bananas peeled, split, and sauced as needed.

| Ginger root, fresh, peeled | 2-inch piece | Wash the ginger root and smash with a meat mallet or the side of a heavy cleaver. Add to the banana and coconut milk mixture, and place over very low heat, stirring occasionally, until the liquid becomes very creamy. The mixture should have the consistency of thin pudding. If too thick, add more coconut milk. If too thin, simmer a bit longer. |
| Molasses | to taste | Remove the ginger root and add molasses to taste. Pour into individual dessert dishes or cups and refrigerate until needed. |

Garnish with grated fresh coconut.

RUM CUSTARD   *Jamaica*

Yield: 10 servings

Milk	1 qt.	Place milk in the upper pot of a double boiler. (Take care that the water in the lower pot does not touch the bottom of the upper one.) Bring the milk to a boil, then lower heat to a simmer. In a separate mixing bowl combine the eggs, sugar, and cornstarch with a wire whisk. Add this mixture to the hot milk; do not allow to boil at this point. Cook, stirring, until the mixture thickens. Remove from heat and add the rum. Pour into individual ramekins or wine glasses and chill.
Eggs, beaten	10	
Sugar, brown	2–3 oz.	
Cornstarch	2 tbsp.	
Rum, dark	4 oz.	
Heavy cream, whipped	as needed	On the top of each serving, pipe slightly sweetened whipped cream laced with a little rum and sprinkle lightly with crushed nuts.
Rum	as needed	
Almonds, toasted and crushed	as needed	

A SHORT PASTRY DOUGH   *Latin America*

Yield: one 11-inch tart shell (8–10 servings)

Flour, all-purpose	8 oz.
Sugar	1 tbsp.
Salt	¾ tsp.
Butter *or* vegetable shortening, chilled and cut in small pieces	6 oz.

Place the flour, sugar, and salt in the bowl of a food processor and blend by using the pulsing action 3–4 times. Add butter or shortening to flour. Pulse until the mixture has the texture of coarse crumbs.

Egg	1
Milk *or* water	1 tbsp.
Vanilla extract	1 tsp.
Nutmeg, grated	½ tsp.

Beat the egg together with the milk or water, vanilla, and nutmeg. With the processor running continuously, add this to the flour mixture. As soon as the dough forms a ball, remove it from the processor. Place the dough on a piece of plastic wrap and shape it into a flat disk about ½ inch thick. Wrap well and refrigerate for at least 1 hour before using.

Butter, softened	as needed
Dry beans	as needed

Lightly butter an 11-inch tart pan, preferably one with a removable bottom. Lightly flour a cold surface (marble is best), and roll out the disk into an even round (1½–2 inches larger than the tart pan).

Roll the dough up onto the rolling pin and transfer it to the tart pan. Gently lift the edges of the dough and press it into the pan, taking care not to stretch the dough. You may remove the excess dough by passing the rolling pin over the top edge of the tart pan. If you wish to make a thicker rim, trim the excess dough so that the overhang is uniform, then turn the excess dough under, making a double thickness of dough along the rim. After the dough has been turned under, place your thumbs on the inside of the rim and your index fingers on the outside of the tart pan. Gently compress the dough while pushing the dough upward along the rim

(Continued)

of the tart pan to slightly increase the height of the rim and give the tart more depth.

Line the dough with aluminum foil and add enough beans to cover the surface to ½ the depth of the pan. Bake in a 375 degree F oven for 15–20 minutes. Remove the foil with the beans and continue to bake for another 5 minutes, or until the bottom of the tart shell feels dry to the touch and is slightly browned. Remove from heat and let cool.

FRESH COCONUT TART   *French Caribbean*

Yield: 8–10 servings

Milk	24 oz.

In a heavy-bottomed saucepan, scald the milk over low to medium heat.

Sugar	8 oz.
Cornstarch	4 tbsp.

In a mixing bowl, blend the sugar and cornstarch thoroughly, then gradually add the hot milk and stir until smooth.

Egg yolks, beaten (whites reserved)	4
Lime peel	1 lime

In a separate mixing bowl, beat the egg yolks. Gradually add the milk and mix well.

Transfer this mixture to the top of a double boiler set over boiling water. Add the lime peel and cook, stirring constantly, until the mixture thickens. Remove the lime peel and discard.

Coconut, fresh, shredded	6 oz.
Butter	2 oz.
Vanilla	1½ tsp.

Remove from heat and add the coconut, butter, and vanilla. Mix well, let cool, and pour into a prebaked 11-inch tart shell.

Egg whites	4
Salt	½ tsp.
Sugar	2 oz.

Beat egg whites and salt together until the egg whites begin to become stiff. Gradually add the sugar and continue beating until the egg whites form stiff peaks. Using a pastry bag, pipe the meringue in an attractive pattern over the top of the tart and bake in a 425 degree F oven for 5–6 minutes, or until lightly browned.

FRESH MANGO TART *Caribbean*

Yield: 8–10 servings

Mangoes, ripe, peeled and sliced thin	1½ lb. (5–6 whole mangoes)
Sugar	6 oz.
Water	6 oz.
Cinnamon stick	2-inch piece

Combine the mangoes, sugar, water, and cinnamon in a saucepan and bring to a boil. Lower heat to simmer and cook for 15 minutes, stirring frequently. When done, remove the mango mixture from the heat and discard the cinnamon stick. Let cool slightly.

Egg yolks	3
Water	2 oz.
Cornstarch	2 tbsp.
Sugar	if needed
Lemon juice, fresh squeezed	to taste

Combine the egg yolks, water, and cornstarch and whisk into a smooth paste. Add this to the mango mixture and, stirring quickly, blend thoroughly. Return the saucepan to the heat and cook over low heat, stirring, until the mixture has thickened. Add sugar, if needed, and lemon juice to taste.

Pour into an unbaked 11-inch tart shell and bake in a 350 degree F oven for 20–30 minutes, or until the mango mixture is firm. Let cool before serving.

Top with unsweetened, whipped cream.

BANANA COCONUT TART *Cuba*

Yield: 8–10 servings

Milk	24 oz.

In a heavy-bottomed saucepan, scald the milk over low to medium heat.

Sugar	8 oz.
Cornstarch	4 tbsp.

In a mixing bowl, blend the sugar and cornstarch thoroughly, then gradually add the hot milk and stir until smooth.

(Continued)

Egg yolks, beaten	4

In a separate mixing bowl, beat the egg yolks. Gradually add the milk and mix well. Transfer this mixture to the top of a double boiler set over boiling water. Cook, stirring, until the mixture thickens.

Coconut, fresh, shredded	3 oz.

Remove from heat and add the coconut. Stir well, let cool a bit, and reserve.

Pastry shell, partially baked	one 11-inch shell
Bananas	as needed

Slice bananas thin and arrange them to cover the bottom of a prebaked, cooled pastry shell. Ladle the coconut mixture evenly over the bananas. Wrap in plastic wrap and refrigerate until chilled.

Whipped cream	as needed
Liquor of choice	as needed
Coconut flakes, toasted, or almond slivers, blanched and toasted	as needed

To serve, top portions with slightly sweetened whipped cream that has been flavored with a liquor of choice. Garnish with toasted coconut flakes or blanched and toasted almond slivers.

COCONUT CREAM   *Haiti*

Yield: 10–12 servings

Evaporated milk	24 oz.
Condensed milk	12 oz.
Coconut milk, thick	12 oz.
Vanilla	1 tsp.

Combine the evaporated milk, the condensed milk, and the coconut milk in a heavy sauce pan and bring to a boil. Remove from heat and let cool for five minutes.

Gelatine, unflavored, granulated	4 tbsp.
Water	4 oz.

Sprinkle the gelatine evenly over the water and allow to soften for 2–3 minutes. Then add to the warm milk mixture and stir well. Pour into individual serving custard cups or goblets and chill until set.

Garnish with shredded coconut that has browned in butter and sugar or any combination of pureed, fresh fruits. This recipe may also be placed in a decorative mold. When chilled and firm, slice and place over fruit puree. Garnish with mint leaves and shredded coconut.

WHIPPED AVOCADO
Latin America

Yield: 10 servings

Avocados, ripe	5
Heavy cream	2 – 3 oz.

Slice each avocado lengthwise into two equal parts. Remove the pulp and place into the bowl of an electric mixer. Reserve the shells. Add the heavy cream. Using the wire whip attachment, mix on high speed until very smooth.

Confectioner's sugar	to taste
Lime juice	to taste

Add the sugar and lime juice to taste. Mix well, then chill before serving.

To serve, pipe or spoon whipped avocado mixture into the reserved shells or into an appropriate dessert goblet. Garnish with a rosette of whipped cream.

FLAN   *Mexico*

Yield: 10 servings

Caramel:

Sugar	12 oz.
Water	4 oz.
Chili pepper, red, dried	1
Butter	as needed

Combine the sugar, water, and chili pepper in a small, heavy pan over low to medium heat, stirring constantly. Cook, until the mixture is honey-colored and has the consistency of syrup, about 8 – 10 minutes. Remove from heat, discard the chili pepper, and pour equal amounts into 10 oven-proof custard cups. Twirl cups to distribute caramel evenly around the bottoms of the cups. When cool, spread a light coating of butter on the portions of the custard cups that are not covered by the caramel.

Flan:

Milk	1 qt.
Sugar	8 oz.
Eggs	8
Vanilla	2 tsp.

Combine these ingredients in a blender and mix for 1 minute on medium speed. Pour mixture into the custard cups which have been placed on a rack on a baking pan. Fill the pan halfway up the sides of the cups with water that is just below the boiling point. Bake in a 375 degree F

(Continued)

oven for 30–40 minutes or until the custard is set. Test to see if done by inserting a toothpick or small knife into one of the custards. If it comes out clean the custard is done. Remove from heat and let cool. To serve, place on individual dessert plates, and unmold. If the flan is refrigerated, it may be necessary to run a thin knife around the sides or to immerse the cups briefly in hot water to unmold and release the caramel.

SUGGESTED READINGS

Asociación de Damas Peruano-Panamenas. *Las Mejores Recetas De Cocina*. Panama: 1989.

Bayless, Rick, with Deann Groen Bayless. *Authentic Mexican*. New York: William Morrow and Company, Inc., 1987.

Brown, Cora, Rose, and Bob. *The South American Cookbook*. New York: Dover Publications, Inc., 1971.

Burt, Elinor. *Olla Podrida*. Caldwell, Idaho: The Claxton Printers, Ltd., 1941.

Cadwallader, Sharon. *Savoring Mexico*. San Francisco: Chronicle Books, 1987.

Creen, Linette. *A Taste of Cuba*. New York: Dutton, 1991.

De Billingslea, Dora. *100 Recetas Típicas Panamenas De Doña Dora*. Barcelona: Lider Editores, S.A.

Del Real, Maria Eloisa Alverez. *Cocina Latinoamericana*. Panama: Editorial America, S.A.

De Ortuno, Julia. *Libro De Cocina*. Honduras.

Davila, Vivian. *Puerto Rican Cooking*. Secaucus, New Jersey: Castle Books, 1988.

De Andrade, Margarette. *Brazilian Cookery*. Rio de Janeiro: A Casa Do Livro Eldorado, 1987.

Dedeaux, Devra. *The Sugar Reef Caribbean Cookbook*. New York: Dell Publishing, 1989.

Elbert, Verginie F. and George A. *Down-Island Caribbean Cookery*. New York: Simon and Schuster, 1991.

Gabilondo, Aida. *Mexican Family Cooking*. New York: Fawcett Columbine, 1986.

Harris, Dunstan A. *Island Cooking: Recipes from the Caribbean*. Freedom, California: The Crossing Press, 1988.

Harris, Jessica B. *Iron Pots and Wooden Spoons*. New York: Battantine Books, 1989.

Harris, Jessica B. *Sky Juice and Flying Fish*. New York: Fireside, 1991.

Karoff, Barbara. *South American Cooking*. Berkeley, California: Aris Books, 1989.

Kennedy, Diana. *The Art of Mexican Cooking*. New York: Bantam Books, 1989.

Marks, Copeland. *False Tongues and Sunday Bread*. New York: M. Evans and Company, Inc., 1985.

Ortiz, Elizabeth Lambert. *The Complete Book of Caribbean Cooking*. New York: Ballantine Books, 1973.

Ortiz, Elizabeth Lambert. *The Book of Latin American Cooking*. New York: Vintage Books, 1979.

Peyton, James W. *El Norte: The Cuisine of Northern Mexico*. Santa Fe, New Mexico: Red Crane Books, 1990.

Rojas-Lombardi, Felipe. *The Art of South American Cooking*. New York: HarperCollins Publishers, 1991.

Schley, Vicki Barrios and Angelo Villa. *Mexican Cooking*. California Culinary Academy. San Francisco: Ortho Books, Chevron Chemical Company.

Schneider, Elizabeth. *Uncommon Fruits and Vegetables: A Commonsense Guide*. New York: Harper and Row Publishers, Inc., 1986.

Schweid, Richard. *Hot Peppers*. Louisiana: New Orleans School of Cooking, 1987.

Sierra Franco de Alvarez, Aurora. *Cocina Regional Guatemalteca*. Guatemala, American Central: Editorial Piedra Santa, 1989.

Springer, Rita G. *Caribbean Cookbook*. London: Pan Books, Ltd., 1979.

Valldejuli, Carmen Aboy. *Puerto Rican Cookery*. Gretna, Louisiana: Pelican Publishing Company, Inc., 1977.

Willinsky, Helen. *Jerk Barbecue from Jamaica*. Freedom, California: The Crossing Press, 1990.

INDEX

West Lafayette Public Library
West Lafayette, Indiana